Darrel Gabbard has done it once again. The Unique Supremacy of Jesus is biblical, practical, and applicable in everyday life. As he offers an insightful examination of the seven, " I AM" statements in the Gospel of John, Darrel not only proves the unique supremacy of Jesus, but also the authenticity of Jesus. What an incredible foundation that has been laid for a potential sermon series or small group study. Do yourself a favor and order this book today!

Dr. Jeremy Westbrook, Executive Director - Treasurer
State Convention of Baptists in Ohio

Pastor Darrel Gabbard, led by the Holy Spirit, has put together in one book, years of preaching and teaching about Jesus and why Jesus is the great I AM. There are seven great, easy-to-read chapters in "The Unique Supremacy of Jesus" to prove this point. Reading this book was like I was back in the congregation listening to one of his sermons again. Darrel always makes his point in a simple and easy to understand way, then backs it up with multiple verses from the Bible. Throughout the book he always gives people a chance to accept Jesus as Lord and Savior or grow as a believer to become a better person and disciple. Darrel, thank you for all the years of growing my family and myself in Christ. May the Lord continue to use you in a mighty way.

Michael Stasko, Founder and CEO
Sunny Street Cafe
Best Restaurant Equipment & Design, Inc.
Deacon, Dublin Baptist Church, Dublin, Ohio

This book represents the overall focus of Darrel's entire preaching ministry. He effectively encourages and equips us with the truths of Christ's uniqueness. You will grow deeper in your love for Christ, and stronger in your witness for Him.

Rev. Randall Wood, Senior Pastor
Midway Baptist Church, Columbus, North Carolina

I am thankful for Darrel's work around the 'I Am' statements of Jesus. It's a reminder to my soul that because He is the Great I Am, I can relax in the reality that 'I am not.' I hope you read this book!

Rev. Dean Fulks, Senior Pastor
LifePoint Church, Lewis Center, Ohio

The Unique Supremacy of Jesus is a clear, concise, and compelling call to embrace Jesus as Lord and Savior! The author - my dear friend and pastor - systematically, with Biblical and theological accuracy, declares Jesus as the Son of God and Son of Man who desires to be our Lord and Savior and above all receive our praise, honor, and glory as the Great I Am!

Dr. Paul L. H. Olson
Retired Corporate & University Executive
Former NFL Player

The Unique Supremacy of Jesus

by

Darrel Gabbard

FBS Publications

Columbus, Ohio

─────────── ∿ ───────────

Cover photo by James Frie

─────────── ∿ ───────────

Printed in the United States of America

First Printing, 2024

ISBN 97-983-2042211-4

─────────── ∿ ───────────

FBS Publications
Columbus, Ohio

Table of Contents

Dedication

Dedicated to our beautiful daughter

Kimberly Anne Collins.

She has a strong character but also a tender heart.

She serves her husband Scott and her elderly parents with a selfless devotion.

And most importantly she loves Jesus!

She helped me tremendously as I wrote this book.

Her mother and I are so grateful that God blessed us with the privilege of being her parents.

Introduction: A Personal Testimony

THE UNIQUE SUPREMACY OF JESUS

At the time of this writing, I am a 78-year-old retired pastor with some health challenges. I have written one other book (JOSEPH: A Life Shaped for God's Glory), but I have felt compelled to write a book about the One who saved my soul and gave me a reason for living. This One's name is Jesus.

The purpose of this book is to both inform people about Jesus and to celebrate His gospel (Good News). It is my prayer that this focus on the supremacy and uniqueness of Jesus will give fresh assurance and excitement to those who already know Him, and that they in turn will share it with friends and family who have never experienced His transforming power in their own lives.

I want to begin by sharing my own story. From the time I was a small boy the name "Jesus" was a very familiar name in the family in which I grew up. My mother was blessed with a devout Christian background. Her maternal grandfather was a Methodist circuit riding preacher in the hills of Kentucky. This meant that he traveled a specifically assigned circuit on horseback each Sunday to preach the gospel of Jesus in small Methodist churches. He had a profound impact upon my grandmother, who was one of the godliest women I have ever known. She loved Jesus with all her heart. Her name is Maud Jones. My mother's father died when she was 10 years old. He was a Baptist, and so eventually my grandmother joined what they called a Missionary Baptist Church. She raised my mother (Oskie), along with an older sister (Iris), and brother (Clark) by herself, choosing not to get remarried. The primary reason was because my mother's brother was struck as a teenager with a significant disability. My grandmother gave of herself in selfless devotion to take care of her disabled son. This was rooted, of course, in her love for her son, but also in her great love and devotion to Jesus.

My mother would eventually move to Ohio as a young adult to be near her older sister who had married and settled in Cincinnati. She moved north to look for work and found a job in Hamilton, Ohio that resulted in her meeting Hugh Gabbard whose first wife had died. They eventually got married and ten months later I was born. My dad believed in God, but he had never had a personal life changing encounter with Jesus. When I was around seven years old, a nephew of my grandmother came to preach in a series of revival meetings at Emanuel Baptist Church in Hamilton, Ohio. Since dad knew this relative, he decided to go to a service and while there he had a life changing encounter with Jesus. He decided to follow Jesus, and his life was dramatically transformed. From this point on we were in church every Sunday. Dad would eventually be ordained a deacon. My parents would later become involved in the planting of two new SBC churches: first in Hamilton, Ohio (Southern Hills Baptist Church) and then secondly in Fairfield, Ohio (First Baptist Church). My dad and mom loved singing and playing gospel music. They would join up with a soprano and a tenor, and mom sang alto, and to quote Johnny Cash, "daddy sang bass". Singing about Jesus was a priority in my family.

2

At the age of nine, I was sitting in a Sunday evening worship service, and I actually found myself listening to what the pastor was saying. I felt a tug at my heart that convinced me that Jesus was calling me to receive Him as my Lord and Savior. After the service I told my parents about what I had experienced that evening. They set up a time for me to meet with our pastor. I don't recall what he said to me, but after having met with him I went away with an assurance that Jesus had come into my heart. Later at the age of ten, I publicly professed my faith in Jesus through baptism by immersion (by Pastor F.C. Tuttle).

From that time on, I had a sensitive heart to who Jesus is and what he had planned for my life. I don't mean to imply that I was a "little angel". I could be "ornery" sometimes, but by the grace of God, I always had a desire to please my parents and the Lord Jesus. Throughout my teenage years, again by God's grace, I stayed active in my church. There were a lot of godly men who took an interest in me and were great role models. Their authentic love for Jesus inspired me. At the age of 18, I went to Miami University in Oxford, Ohio unsure of what to pursue as far as a career. I commuted from home in Fairfield, Ohio while attending Miami. This enabled me to still attend my home church as well as to do some part-time work which helped pay my tuition. As I continued my studies at Miami I began to struggle with some restlessness. I had initially chosen to major in Systems Analysis, but it was clear to me that this was not my "thing". During this time, I also encountered some secular ideas that challenged my faith. Rather than causing me to seriously doubt my belief in Jesus, it forced me to reexamine my faith with an openness to truth. During this period, I began to test what I believed and why I believed it. This resulted in an even deeper conviction about the reliability of the scriptures and the claims it made about Jesus. I had a new conviction about what I believed and why I believed it.

Also at this time, I began to sense that tug at my heart once again from Jesus. Others, including my Grandma Jones, had told me that they saw in me a possible call to be a minister of the Gospel. The thought of standing before people preaching the Word of God petrified me. I had always been a bit shy and even tended to behave like an introvert. But I experienced a growing conviction and desire to share the Word of God and so during the fall revival at my home church, I felt compelled at the time of the altar call to go to the front and share with my pastor and church family that I knew God was calling me to be a minister of the Gospel. I knew that the Spirit of God had touched my heart with a passion to serve Jesus and preach His Gospel. It was very emotional for me. I cried like a baby. But these were not tears of sadness but of tremendous joy and relief. My pastor, Bob Bateman, was a true man of God. His love for Jesus was contagious, and God used him as a role model and great encourager. The congregation also greatly encouraged me and affirmed my calling to be a minister of the gospel.

For the next three years I continued my studies at Miami majoring in history. I worked three summers at a paper mill and one summer for the city of Fairfield. I also worked on Saturdays for a building contractor who was a friend of our family. It was all physical labor, and so I have joked over the years that those jobs helped confirm my calling to be a minister of the gospel. Also, during this time I would do supply preaching in SBC churches in southwestern Ohio. I continued to read Christian authors to help me better understand the basic doctrines of the Christian faith. I remember one summer sitting in our back yard reading a book by Billy Graham titled "Peace with God". And for the first time I was gripped by the glorious doctrine called "Justification by faith". My love and devotion for Jesus took a big step of growth that day. I had heard the term often used in church and believed it, but I had never understood the full implications it had for believers in Jesus. I was so thrilled that when I got up to return to our house, I found myself physically leaping for joy.

Another source of great joy was meeting my bride to be. While still commuting to Miami as I approached my senior year, I had dated a few Christian girls, but no serious relationship had developed. But one Sunday morning, as I was singing with the choir during the public invitation for people to come forward to decide for Christ, I saw a beautiful young lady come down the aisle. At the time, I must confess, I was not focusing on her spiritual needs. After our pastor announced that Brenda Everidge had come to transfer her membership, I was thrilled. Well, it took a while for the two of us to connect because she was dating another guy. But I am convinced the Lord had already preordained our connection. She was not only beautiful on the outside, but she had a beautiful heart for Jesus. She had sensed that the Lord was calling her into some form of full time ministry. Not long after she joined our church, she broke up with the other guy and I "prayerfully" made my move. After graduating from Miami University in 1967 with a B. A. degree, Brenda and I were married in July, and then immediately moved to Louisville, Kentucky to attend the Southern Baptist Theological Seminary. I graduated from the seminary in 1970 with an M. Div. degree. God granted me great favor with the privilege of pastoring five SBC churches from 1968 until my retirement in 2013 due to health issues. My last pastorate was at Dublin Baptist Church in Dublin, Ohio where I served for 24 ½ years as Senior (Lead) Pastor. Later the church elected me as Pastor Emeritus.

I must add that making a commitment to be a follower of Jesus does not mean one's life becomes easier or pain free. Jesus told his followers "I have said these things to you, that in me you may have peace, In the world you will have tribulation, but take heart; I have overcome the world." (John16:33) During the course of all these years of ministry, Brenda and I have certainly faced tribulation. Brenda has had numerous health issues. Some have been very debilitating. But through it all she has demonstrated a strong persevering faith. Her determination has been an inspiration for me.

The most devastating experiences we have had were the deaths of our two sons. Our youngest son, Kevin, after struggling for years with depression, chose to end his life at the age of 32 in the Spring of 2006. From the time he was in grade school he struggled. There is no need to go into the details, but we did all we could do to try to help him. And then in 2020, our oldest child Christopher died at age 50 due to heart failure and diabetes. It is hard to put into words the grief one feels when your children precede you in death. But as intense as the grief was, the comfort and peace we received through our faith in Jesus, God's grace was even more powerful. To paraphrase the words of the apostle Paul, "I can do (handle or face) all things through Christ who strengthens me" (Philippians 4:13).

After retirement, I continued to serve Jesus in a part time position with the Metro Columbus Baptist Association as Pastoral Encourager for 8 years. This position basically involved being a "Barnabas" to pastors. I would meet pastors treating them to lunch or breakfast, and to basically listen, encourage and be a friend. I greatly enjoyed this ministry. But I was diagnosed several years ago with a form of Parkinson's called Parkinsonism. This has made it increasingly difficult for me to safely get around on my own, and so I now need a walker. It has also affected my ability to speak, and so I am no longer able to preach. I struggle with projecting my voice with enough volume, and I have lost some of my ability to pronounce words with clarity.

But I am still trying to serve my Lord through writing. Also, I text and call friends and family to encourage them if they are struggling with some issue. We also pray for the missionaries to whom we give financial support to assist their evangelistic work for Jesus locally, nationally and internationally.

I cannot imagine what my life would have been like without having met Jesus. By His grace and mercy, I have experienced a life of incredible blessing. But as I have already indicated, this does not mean, that the followers of Jesus can live in this world without dealing with some pain and suffering. The Bible teaches that we live in a fallen sinful world. We humans are rebels and out of our defiance of God, we have brought pain, suffering and death upon ourselves.

But despite our rebellion, Jesus, the one and only Son of God, came to this earth on a rescue mission. Who He is and what He accomplished is what the Bible calls the gospel, or the good news.

As David Jeremiah has written, "Someone once said, 'Just give me Jesus!' Give me Jesus Himself—the Jesus of Scripture, the Jesus of history, the Son of Man from heaven, the Son of God who rules and reigns. He is the incomparable and indescribable enigma of history. We have trouble describing Jesus because He is indescribable. Yet in John's Gospel, Jesus managed to define Himself perfectly in the simplest of terms ever—two little words totaling three letters---"I AM".

The title of this book, "The Unique Supremacy of Jesus", is a good summation of the book's focus. There has never been, nor will there ever be another person walk upon this earth who is comparable to Jesus. He is unique indeed. And the phrase "I AM", when understood, best captures His identity and His supremacy.

The Gospel of John records twenty-two occasions when Jesus used this phrase in reference to Himself. The Greek version of the phrase is "ego eimi". This is the Greek equivalent of the Hebrew name that God used to identify Himself when He spoke to Moses at the burning bush. This sets us up for the first chapter titled "The Great I AM"

One

"The Great I Am"

John 8:48-59

Key verse: "Jesus said to them, 'Truly, truly, I say to you, before Abraham was, I am.'" (John 8:58 ESV)

In his book, "The Bush is Still Burning", Dr. Lloyd Ogilvie told of an interesting encounter he had one day with a man who had been seeing him occasionally for counseling. Having talked with the man a few times he felt free to ask a penetrating question. Dr. Ogilvie asked him, "What do you now feel is the greatest need in your life, and what can I do to help?" The man's immediate response was, "I need a new God!" Dr. Ogilvie was a bit taken back, and so the man went on to explain. "During the times we have met the past few weeks, we have been talking about the struggles in my life. You have tried to tell me about how God loves me, and that He has the desire and ability to help me get through my struggles. That has been difficult for me to hear, because even though I have been exposed to all of this, it hit me the other day that what I really need is a new God. I have apparently had a lot of mistaken and distorted ideas about God."

He went on to describe how he had always seen God as sort of like an absentee landlord, aloof, distant, and non-existent as far as daily problems are concerned. But Dr. Ogilvie had described to the man a different God, so the man concluded, "My greatest need is to find this new God, not new in the sense that he never existed before, but new to me."

I believe that this man's need reflects the needs of many people I encounter in today's secularized culture. The reason so many people struggle with the challenges of trying to survive in our modern world is because they also need a new God. Many people have unknowingly chosen to worship false secularized gods, while others know about the true God, but they have never really had a life changing encounter with Him.

A lot of people have settled for a small god of their own making. But every human being's greatest need is to enter a personal relationship with the true God who is the awesome creator, sustainer and savior of the universe. This great and awesome God is ever present and powerful, and He makes things happen. He knows each of us by name, and preordained our existence even before we were conceived in our mother's womb. This God is the one and only true God who may be new to some who are reading this book right now. But how do we meet and get to know such an overwhelming Person? Well, this is the focus of this book.

The passage I mentioned earlier makes clear how this has been made possible. It is my prayer that as you read this book you will get to know the true God through a life changing encounter with Jesus.

The setting for this encounter Jesus had with the Jewish leaders was the Temple in Jerusalem during the Feast of Tabernacles. This was the last of the seven annual feasts that devout Jews celebrated each year to commemorate God's provision for His people during their wanderings in the wilderness.

Prior to this critical moment, we read earlier that this specific group of Jews had a favorable impression of Jesus. But when Jesus told them that they needed to be set free from sin, they were offended and turned against Him.   They assumed that since they were physical descendants of Abraham, they were not in need of this liberation to which Jesus had referred. They had been taught that as sons of Abraham they were automatically children of God. Notice in verse 48 they even accused Jesus of having a demon. Look at John 8:48-58. What a radical statement, especially to a group of Jewish leaders! They thought they had Jesus all figured out. But this claim that Jesus made about Himself confronted them with a decision. Would they be open to a new understanding of God? When Jesus said, "Before Abraham was, I Am", He was revealing several amazing truths about Himself; truths that confronted these Jewish leaders with a new fuller revelation of God which they were not prepared to accept.

First, this "I Am" statement revealed:

HIS IDENTITY

JESUS CLAIMED TO BE THE GOD WHO REVEALED HIMSELF TO MOSES

I am sure that most of those reading this book are familiar with the Old Testament story of Moses. He was born in Egypt to Hebrew parents during a time when God's chosen people were suffering horrific oppression. There was an earlier time when the Hebrews flourished in this pagan land. This was after Joseph had been used by God to rise from the position of a slave to a deliverer of the Egyptian people through his ability to interpret dreams. God gave him an ability to interpret the dreams of Pharaoh. He had foreseen in the King's dream that for the next seven years the Egyptians would have seven years of abundant crops followed by seven years of drought. The King believed Joseph's interpretation as well as Joseph's suggestion that they store up extra grain during the time of abundance, and therefore have an adequate supply ready when the seven years of drought came.

Pharaoh was so impressed with Joseph, he placed Joseph in charge of this massive project.

Well, the plan worked perfectly. The Egyptians flourished despite the drought, as did the Hebrews. God's people remained in Egypt for 400 years multiplying into a great nation. We read in the first chapter of the book of Exodus that a new king arose over Egypt who was not familiar with Joseph and the history of the Hebrew people. This new Pharaoh became concerned about the rapid growth of the children of Israel. He said to his leaders and people, "look at how quickly these people are multiplying". He saw them as a threat. Look at what this new Pharaoh said in Exodus 1:9-10 (ESV), "And he said to his people, 'Behold, the people of Israel are too many and too mighty for us. Come, let us deal shrewdly with them, lest they multiply, and, if war breaks out, they join our enemies and fight against us and escape from the land." And so, this new Pharaoh implemented a plan in which he basically made the Hebrews into slaves with harsh taskmasters overseeing their work. Their tasks consisted of the building of two "store" cities called Pithos and Ramses, as well as working in the fields. It was ruthless hard labor. Then this evil king took the oppression to another level when he demanded that the Hebrew midwives kill all the baby boys who were born. But the midwives refused to engage in such atrocities. Then Pharoah commanded all his people to cast every son born to the Hebrews into the Nile.

This leads us to the story of Moses' birth. Exodus chapter two relates the story of a Levite woman who gave birth to a beautiful baby boy. She hid him for three months, but when she could no longer hide him, she made a basket out of bulrushes and put her precious son in the basket and then placed it among the reeds by the Nile riverbank. The sister of Moses stood at a distance to observe what would happen. Through the sovereign work of God, the daughter of Pharaoh came down to bathe in the river and as she walked by the river, she saw the basket among the reeds, and sent her servant woman to go secure the basket. When she opened the basket, the child was crying, and the servant woman felt compassion for him and said, "This is one of the Hebrew's children". Then Moses' sister, who was standing nearby, suggested to Pharoah's daughter, "Shall I go and call you a nurse from the Hebrew women, to come and nurse the child for you?". The King's daughter agreed, and so immediately the girl intentionally went to enlist Moses' mother. And Pharoah's daughter said, "Take this child away and nurse him for me, and I will give you wages". And this is what she did, and when the child grew up, she brought him to Pharoah's daughter, and he officially became the son of the King's daughter. She named him Moses, "because", she said, "I drew him out of water." The name "Moses" sounds like the Hebrew word for "draw out".

I share this story in detail because we see the sovereign hand of God in the entire story. None of this happened by accident. And this foreshadows another even more amazing story of the birth of the Christ child named Jesus.

Moses grew up as an Egyptian prince. But keep in mind that until he was around 12 years old, his Hebrew mother had a lot of influence on him. And so, he had some familiarity with his Hebrew heritage. As a young adult, it became apparent that he began to identify more and more with the people of his mother's heritage. He began to feel a deep anguish over the plight of the Hebrews. This led to a moment when Moses one day went out to his people to observe their burdens, and while there he saw an Egyptian beating a fellow Hebrew. He felt this terrible rage. After looking around to see if anyone was watching, he attacked and killed the Egyptian taskmaster who had been abusing a Hebrew slave. He then buried the dead man in the sand and fled.

The next day Moses discovered that others had observed his crime, and that Pharoah was informed. The word was out that the king was planning to track down Moses and have him executed. So, Moses fled from Egypt and ended up in the land of Midian. He sat down next to a well. As he sat there, the seven daughters of the priest of Midian came along and filled their troughs to water their father's flocks. But at that moment some shepherds came along and attempted to drive them away, but Moses intervened and saved them.

When the daughters came home to their father Reuel (also known as Jethro), he asked them, "How is it that you have come home so soon today?" They proceeded to tell him about this Egyptian man who intervened and delivered them out of the hands of the shepherds and even drew water for them and watered their flock. Reuel was so appreciative, he invited Moses to stay with them and Moses accepted this gracious invitation. Reuel also gave his daughter Zipporah to Moses to be his wife, after which she gave birth to a son. Moses would remain in the wilderness for forty years, not knowing that this experience was all a part of God's plan to prepare him to someday return to Egypt as God's instrument "through whom He would set His people free from their bondage and lead them to their promised land."

While growing up a prince in Pharoah's pagan kingdom, I'm certain that his birth mother, whom the King's daughter had enlisted to be his tutor, taught him a lot about his Hebrew heritage. He was no doubt familiar with names such as Abraham, Isaac and Jacob. During his years in the desert, he must have pondered some questions, such as: Where is this God of my forefathers now? Does he know about what is happening to His people? Does He care? If He does, why doesn't he do something?

Then one day, after having spent 40 years in the desert as a sheepherder for his father-in-law, the God of his forefathers (Abraham, Isaac and Jacob) spoke to Moses in an audible voice. Moses was keeping the flock of Jethro (Reuel), his father-in-law. He led the flock to the west side of the wilderness and came to Horeb, often called the Mountain of God. This mountain would also be called Mount Sinai. Suddenly the Angel of the Lord appeared to him in a flame of fire out the midst of the bush. He looked and was amazed to see that the bush was burning, yet it was not consumed. Moses said, "I will turn aside to see this great sight, why the bush is not burned (or consumed)" When the Lord saw that Moses had turned aside and gazed upon the bush, He called to him out of the bush and said, "Moses, Moses!" And Moses simply replied, saying, "Here I am." Then the Lord instructed Moses not to come near, and to also take off his sandals because he was standing on holy ground. After this, the Lord informed Moses, "I am the God of your father, the God of Abraham, the God of Isaac, and the God of Jacob." And then we are told that Moses hid his face, because he was afraid to look at God. After this, God told Moses that he was very much aware of the suffering of His people, and that He would deliver them out of their bondage in Egypt and lead them back to a land that he had promised to his forefathers. But then the Lord shocked Moses by informing him that He had chosen him to be the one who would deliver his people from their bondage and into this land of great promise.

Well Moses was very reluctant and fearful when he contemplated such an overwhelming task. But God assured him that He would be with Moses and give him the power and ability to accomplish his great task. But Moses came up with a very good question, for He asked God, "Who am I that I should go to Pharoah and bring the children of Israel out of Egypt?". The answer that Moses received introduced him to a new understanding of God regarding his own struggles and the struggles of his people. Look at Exodus 3:12, God said, "But I will be with you, and this shall be the sign for you, that I have sent you: when you have brought the people out of Egypt, you shall serve God on this mountain." Moses asked God another great question. He asked, "If I come to the people of Israel and say to them, 'The God of your fathers has sent me to you,' and they ask me, 'What is his name?' What shall I say to them?". God said to Moses, "I AM WHO I AM." And He said, "Say this to the people of Israel, I AM has sent me to you."

This was historically the first time in which God revealed His personal name. The Hebrew language is not written with vowels, so it is very difficult to sometimes understand the correct pronunciation. God's personal name is transliterated as YHWH. Most believe that the proper pronunciation is Yahweh. Now, some older translations translated YHWH as "Jehovah" or "LORD". The name stems from the Hebrew word which means "to be". So, it literally means "He Who Is". His name expresses that God is self-existent, eternal, and that He is the source of everything else that exists. He always has been, and He always will be. He had no beginning, and He has no end. Some theologians or philosophers have used phrases such as the "unmoved mover" or the "uncaused Cause". But these are too impersonal and static. The great God of the universe is an infinite personal being. And so, His name does not communicate a passiveness but an active involvement in the lives and destiny of His chosen people.

The Hebrew name of Yahweh (Jehovah) includes the concept of action. No longer was the God of Israel to be viewed alone as El-Shaddai, the All-Powerful God or God Almighty; but as Jehovah (Yahweh) or the LORD, who had unlimited power to make things happen in the valley of human struggle.

Well, the LORD did just what He had promised. He empowered Moses to lead His people out of Egyptian bondage. I want you to notice that the LORD's name was almost viewed like a blank check. The LORD said," I Am…" and His people were to fill in the blank according to their need under the LORD's guidance.

The Old Testament tells us that after God revealed His name, Jehovah, it was used in combination with other Hebrew words to express how He would meet the various needs of His people.

Let's consider some these combinations:

• Jehovah Jireh (Genesis 22:14)
  I AM your Provider. ("The LORD Will Provide" ESV)

• Jehovah Shalom (Judges 6:24)
  I AM your Peace. ("The LORD Is Peace" ESV)

- Jehovah Rapha (Exodus 15:26)

  I AM your Healer (or health). ("I am the LORD, your healer" ESV)

- Jehovah Rohi (Psalm 23:1)

  I AM your Shepherd. ("The LORD is my Shepherd" ESV)

- Jehovah Nissi (Exodus 17:15)

  I AM your Banner (or Victory). ("The LORD Is My Banner" ESV)

- Jehovah Tsidkenu (Jeremiah 23:6)

  I AM your Righteousness. ("The LORD is our Righteousness" ESV)

- Jehovah Shammah (Ezekiel 48:35)

  I AM There. ("The LORD is There" ESV)

When Jesus told these Jewish leaders that "Truly, truly, I say to you, before Abraham was, I am.", they immediately responded with outrage, for they correctly understood that He was claiming to be the God of Abraham, who also revealed His name to Moses. They considered this claim to be blasphemy and picked up stones to throw at Him, but it was not the appointed time for Him to die, so He escaped from them and left the temple.

It is interesting that John is the apostle who especially recognized the significance of Jesus using the phrase "I Am" in reference to Himself. David Jeremiah has written "When Jesus kept using the phrase "I Am" to refer to Himself, His critics saw it as tremendous blasphemy; but the apostle John understood it as a tremendous blessing and kept track of it." There can be no doubt that Jesus claimed to be the great "I Am", the eternal Lord of the universe in human flesh.

The Gospel of John records Jesus using the phrase in reference to Himself 22 times. But there are seven specific statements in which Jesus used the phrase "I Am" with a metaphor to help us better understand His unique essence and what He means to us when we respond in faith. But it is one thing for a person to make claims, but it is an entirely different matter to back these claims with evidence. This leads us to consider a second truth about Jesus.

JESUS HAD THE CREDENTIALS TO VERIFY HIS CLAIM

Consider with me the evidence which supports the claim by Jesus that He is the "I Am" who spoke to Moses in the desert.

FIRST, let's consider THE PROPHECIES OF HIS COMING.

In the Old Testament, which was written hundreds of years before Jesus was born, there are at least 60 major prophesies and 270 approximate ramifications in the life of one person. And that person's name is Jesus of Nazareth.

Let's begin by focusing on some examples; hundreds of years before Jesus came to this earth, the Old Testament prophets said that He would come through the lineage of David; that He would miraculously be born of a virgin in the city of David called Bethlehem; that His earthly parents (Joseph and Mary) would have to flee to Egypt to escape Herod's decree that all Jewish baby boys in Bethlehem age two and younger be slaughtered; that His ministry would be preceded by a prophet like Elijah (John the Baptist) to prepare the way for His coming; that He would work miraculous signs and wonders; that He would be betrayed for thirty pieces of silver; that He would die after being nailed to a tree; that His garments would be divided and gambled over; and that He would rise up from the dead. The Old Testament predicted twice that His hands and feet would be pierced, and these words were written 600-800 years before the act of a crucifixion was put into effect by the Romans.

Some have tried to argue that this is all coincidental, but common sense says "no way". Peter Stoner, an expert on the science of probability, has written that by using the science of probability in reference to just eight prophecies being fulfilled in one human being, the chance is one in one hundred quadrillion. This is considering every

18

person who has lived since the time of the prophecy. The evidence is overwhelming; and the only conclusion can be that Jesus of Nazareth was indeed the promised Messiah.

A SECOND credential that affirms that Jesus is the divine Son of God is THE MIRACLE OF HIS BIRTH.

The fact that "He was born of a virgin", after having been miraculously conceived within Mary through the power of God's Holy Spirit, is obviously a unique and incredible event in human history. Look at Matthew 1:18-20; and Luke 1:26-31. The virgin birth affirmed His humanity, because He was born of a woman; and yet it also affirms His deity, for He was conceived of the Holy Spirit. He was indeed both God and man.

The supernatural events surrounding His birth were also evidence that He is indeed the Messiah. These events include the appearance of the angels; the Magi (Wise men) being led from the far east by a star to the Christ child's residence; and the shepherds responding to the angelic announcement of the Savior's birth and then their short journey to visit the newborn King lying in a manger.

A THIRD credential is THE PERFECTION OF HIS LIFE.

Jesus claimed to be sinless and perfect, and He backed up such a claim by the quality of His life. Those who followed Him as His disciples could not find any flaw or inconsistency in the life He lived before them every day. On one occasion He challenged His enemies with the question, "Which of you convicts me of sin?" (John 8:46). His question was met with silence even though He addressed His question to those who would have loved to point out some flaw in His character.

It is especially striking that John, Peter and Paul, who were all taught from their earliest childhood to believe that all humans were sinners, all spoke of the sinlessness of Christ. In 1 John 3:5, John wrote "In Him is no sin"; in I Peter 2:22, Peter quoted Isaiah 53 in reference to Jesus which says of the coming Messiah, "who did not sin, neither was guile found in His mouth"; and Paul in 2 Corinthians 5:21 simply wrote about Jesus that He "knew no sin". Even Pontius Pilate, who was certainly no friend of Jesus, asked "What evil has he done?" (Matthew 27:23); and concluded by saying "I have found no fault in this man concerning those things of which you accuse him" (Luke 23:14). Jesus was not tried and executed because of any evil deeds He did, but because of who He claimed to be. He claimed to be the Messiah and God the Son which the Jewish leaders considered to be blasphemy. Pilate yielded to the demands of Jewish leaders because he did not want to get in trouble with Caesar due to the possible perception that he may have lost control.

A FOURTH credential which backs His claims is THE AUTHORITY OF HIS TEACHINGS.

When men were sent from Jerusalem to seize Jesus and bring Him before the Sanhedrin (similar to our Supreme Court), they returned without Him. When questioned concerning their failure, they replied in John 7:46, "No man ever spoke like this man!" After Jesus delivered His "Sermon on the Mount", Matthew 7:28-29 records these words, "The people were astonished at his teaching, for he taught them as one having authority, and not as the scribes." Throughout the centuries, people have marveled at the teachings, even including many skeptics. His words are in one sense simple, and yet profound. They have a ring of truth that is very compelling. Through the centuries, millions of people have believed and obeyed His teachings and as a result their lives, including my own, have been transformed.

The FIFTH credential is THE POWER OF HIS WORKS.

Jesus demonstrated an amazing power and authority over the forces of nature, which could belong only to Almighty God, the author and ruler over these forces. For example, He stilled a raging storm of wind and waves on the Sea of Galilee, by simply saying, "Peace, Be still". Immediately, the wind ceased, and the waves calmed down. The disciples were awestruck by what they had just seen and heard. In

Mark 4:41 we read, "And they were filled with great fear and said to one another, 'Who then is this, that even the wind and the waves obey him?'" (ESV) He also demonstrated the Creator's power and authority over sickness and disease. The gospel writers of the New Testament all relate amazing eyewitness accounts of miracles which Jesus performed, such as enabling the lame to walk, the deaf to hear and the blind to see. He even, on three recorded occasions, raised the dead.

Jesus never performed miracles for mere entertainment nor for the purpose of merely showing off. His miracles were intended to be both signs teaching a spiritual truth as well as meeting human need. He came preaching the Good News of the Kingdom of God. His earthly ministry was a glimpse of what the future would be like for all who believe and receive Him. There will be no more death nor sorrow; no more pain nor suffering. His Kingdom will be a paradise delivered from all evil including the devil.

When Nicodemus, the Jewish ruler, arranged to meet secretly with Jesus one evening, he said to Jesus, "...Rabbi, we know that you are a teacher come from God, for no one can do these signs that you do unless God is with him." (John3:2 ESV) I close this section by quoting three important statements Jesus made about His works: John 10:25b (ESV), "The works that I do in my Father's name bear witness about me." John 10:38 (ESV)," ...even though you do not believe me, believe the works, that you may know and understand that the Father is in me and I am in the Father." John 14:11 (ESV), "Believe me that I am in the Father and the Father is in me, or else believe on account of the works themselves."

The SIXTH and most compelling credential of all is THE GLORY OF HIS RESURRECTION.

This is the supreme test about the claims of Christ. According to the historical accounts, recorded in the New Testament, at least five times during His three years of ministry, Jesus predicted that He would die on a Roman cross, and on the third day He would rise from the dead

21

and appear to His disciples. And indeed, He did! On the third day He arose from the dead and over a time period of forty days, Christ appeared to over 500 eyewitnesses in a new, glorified, incorruptible body.

The apostle Paul wrote these amazing words recorded in I Corinthians 15:1,3-10a (ESV) "Now I would remind you, brothers, of the gospel I preached to you, which you received, in which you stand, and by which you are being saved...For I delivered to you as of first importance what I also received: that Christ died for our sins in accordance with the scriptures, that he was buried, that he was raised on the third day in accordance with the scriptures, and that he appeared to Cephas, then to the twelve; Then he appeared to more than five hundred brothers at one time, most of whom are still alive, though some have fallen asleep. Then he appeared to James, to all the apostles. Last of all, as to one untimely born, he also appeared to me".

These credentials provide overwhelming evidence that Jesus was and is the great I Am who spoke to Moses. In fact, look again at what He claimed, as we read earlier in John chapter 8:56-59 (ESV), "Your father Abraham rejoiced to see my day. He saw it and was glad." So, the Jews said to him, 'You are not yet fifty years old and have you seen Abraham?' Jesus said to them, "Truly, truly, I say to you, before Abraham was, I am." So, they picked up stones to throw at him, but Jesus hid himself and went out of the temple."

THIS MEANS THAT JESUS WAS FULLY GOD AND FULLY MAN.

Jesus was the incarnation (in flesh) of God. This truth is fundamental to the Christian faith. He is sometimes called the infinite God-Man. This does not mean that He was part man and part God. He had a dual nature. He did not cease to be God when He became a man, but as a man, God the Son had a human nature apart from sin and lived in dependence upon God the Father. Let us keep in perspective that God is one, yet three in one. He is a Tri-unity (Trinity). He is the Father, the Son and the Holy Spirit. All three persons of the Godhead pre-existed as God, the creator of the universe. This is why Jesus would say that "before Abraham was born, I Am". Abraham was born around 2000 years before Jesus came to this earth.

Remember when God declared His intent to create man, He said in Genesis 1:26," Let us make man in our image, according to our likeness..." This amazing statement reveals to us a conversation which took place among the Godhead prior to the creation of Adam and Eve. Notice that God said, "Let Us". He is conversing with the Son and the Holy Spirit. In essence God is saying "Let Us (Father, Son, and Holy Spirit) make man in Our image, according to Our likeness". This is why Jesus could say, "Before Abraham was (born), I Am". He has always existed as God the Son. But He did not have a human nature until He came to this earth through the virgin birth. Dr. George Truett was quoted as saying, "He was as much man as though he were not God at all; and as much God as though he were not man at all, He was God's perfect man, and man's perfect God."

Now in closing this chapter, I want to briefly mention that the statement Jesus made about being in existence before Abraham, not only reveals HIS IDENTITY, but it also reveals:

HIS ABILITY

BECAUSE OF WHO JESUS IS HE IS ABLE TO MEET OUR NEEDS

This is what God was saying to Moses when He revealed His name to be I AM. As the great I AM of the universe, it was clear that He is All-powerful. Everything that exists derived its being from Him as the Supreme Being. Nothing would be too difficult for Him, including the deliverance of His people from the hands of Pharaoh. His name is Yahweh. He would indeed deliver His people out the of the hands of Pharaoh. Remember the amazing escape when the Egyptian army pursued the Hebrews as they fled from Egypt and they came to the Red Sea. Moses then raised his staff and commanded the people to move forward in faith; as they did, the waters parted and God's people made it across safely, and as Pharaoh's army tried to pursue them the waters collapsed upon their pagan enemies, and Israel was rescued by the great I AM or Yahweh.

But Yahweh's greatest miracle of deliverance happened when He clothed Himself in human flesh, and as the second person of the trinity came to this earth as God the Son, on an incredible rescue mission. The Son of God was given the name of Yeshua or Joshua. It literally means Yahweh saves (or the savior).

The most incredible truth of this story is the means through which He would meet the greatest need, for all who would believe. Jesus (Yahweh clothed in flesh) would go to a horrific cross to suffer and die, taking upon Himself our sins. His body was placed in a tomb, but on the third day He arose from the dead just as He had prophesied. For Moses, Yahweh displayed both His desire and ability to meet the temporal needs of His people, by doing exactly what He had promised Moses He would do. He delivered His suffering people out of their physical bondage. But, through Jesus, Yahweh acted to display both His desire and ability to meet an even greater human need.

He has intervened, through His SON, to pay on our behalf, the penalty for our sins on the cruel Roman cross, to deliver all who would believe out of our spiritual bondage. Jesus (Yeshua) arose from the dead on the third day, proving that He is who He claimed to be and that he has conquered the power of sin and death! John 3:16 sums it up; 'For God so loved the world, that He gave his only Son, that whoever believes in Him should not perish, but have eternal life."

As I close this chapter, I want to appeal to you that if you have never personally trusted in Christ alone as your Lord and Savior, I urge you to do that right now. In John 1:12-13, it says, "But to all who did receive him, who believed in his name, he gave the right to become children of God, who were born, not of blood nor of the will of flesh nor of the will of man, but of God."

Two

"I Am the Bread of Life"

John 6:22-36, 41-51

Key Verses: John 6:35, 48-51 (ESV) "Jesus said to them, 'I am the bread of life; whoever comes to me shall not hunger, and whoever believes in me shall never thirst.... I am the bread of life. Your fathers ate the manna in the wilderness, and they died. This is the bread that comes down from heaven, so that one may eat of it and not die. I am the living bread that came down from heaven. If anyone eats of this bread, he will live forever. And the bread that I will give for the life of the world is my flesh."

Jesus, the divine Son of God, came to meet the deepest needs of the human soul, for the glory of God the Father. His miracles were "signs" designed to reveal those needs and to display how He can meet our needs no matter how difficult they may be. Dr. Lloyd Ogilvie served as chaplain of the U. S. Senate for eight years before he retired. He spoke of a former senator who once said to him, "I feel a dull, persistent ache inside, and it won't go away." I am reminded of the famous words of Augustine who wrote this prayer," O Lord, thou hast created us for thyself and our hearts are restless until they find their rest in thee".

In these statements we find a fundamental truth about life. Everything that exists derives its meaning and significance from God. This is the nature of existence. This truth is inherent in the very fabric of the universe. This is true because of who God is. Remember, God's personal name means "I am".

Because of sin, we humans have been separated from God, which leads to an emptiness and deep spiritual hunger, which nothing in all creation can satisfy except the Creator Himself. This why the study of Jesus, the second Person of the Trinity, is so important. He came to meet the need of every aching, empty soul who is seeking to know Him. And a study of the "I Am" statements can truly illuminate our hearts and minds.

So, let's focus on the meaning and significance of the truth that Jesus is The Bread of Life. Think with me for a moment about what an incredibly astounding statement Jesus made about Himself. In essence Jesus said that what bread is for the physical body, I am for the human soul!! Are you spiritually hungry? Is there a gnawing ache or emptiness deep in your soul? Let's examine in more depth what Jesus taught about the Bread of Life.

1. THE BREAD OF LIFE IS SPIRITUAL IN NATURE

Let us look at the context of what Jesus taught about the Bread of Life. Prior to this teaching we read, beginning in Chapter 6, John's description of the incredible miracle of Jesus feeding the five thousand men, plus the women and children, with a boy's lunch of five barley loaves and two fish. The people were so astounded by this miracle that they sought out Jesus the next day. In verse 26 Jesus said in essence, you have not understood the spiritual lesson of this miracle.

The miracle certainly was performed to meet the physical need of hunger, but it also had another purpose. It was a sign designed to reveal a spiritual truth. The truth is that Jesus alone could meet the needs of human souls that are hungry for spiritual meaning and hope.

Jesus drew a sharp distinction between physical food which is necessary, but only temporal, and the need for spiritual food which He alone could provide. But it was clear that those who were listening could not grasp what Jesus was teaching. Later during the conversation, they referred to the manna which the Lord had provided for their Jewish forefathers, in the wilderness during the Exodus.

Look at John's description in Chapter 6:31, "Our fathers ate the manna in the wilderness; as it is written, 'He gave them bread from heaven to eat.'" Once again Jesus tried to help them understand by saying in verses 32-33, "Truly, truly, I say to you, it was not Moses who gave you the bread from heaven, but my Father gives you the true bread from heaven. For the bread of God is he who comes down from heaven and gives life to the world." No doubt their understanding was still limited, but note their response in verse 34, followed by the amazing claim by Jesus in verse 35; "They said to him, "Sir, give us this bread always." Jesus said to them, "I am the bread of life; whoever comes to me shall not hunger, and whoever believes in me shall never thirst."

Jesus is in essence saying that the greatest need of people is spiritual in nature. We're not just physical beings, but we're also spiritual beings. Just as our bodies need food and water, so do our souls. So many of us tend to focus on what is temporal and perishable. It seems as if most people try to address their problems which have spiritual roots with worldly material solutions. On one occasion, Jesus challenged His disciples with a piercing question; "For what will it profit a man if he gains the whole world and forfeits his own soul?" (Matthew 16:26)

Many parents in our modern culture tend to focus primarily on their children's outward public image and accomplishments, to the neglect of their inner private world, which includes their spiritual needs, their moral values, and the welfare of their souls. After the horrific events associated with the 9/11 terrorist attacks on our country, it appeared that initially the shocking horror and carnage of these events served to be a real wake up call for the American people. Many families began to return to church. A lot of discussions took place in communities about our values as a nation. But after the shock, as time has passed, we see a creeping indifference and even a growing hostility spreading throughout our culture toward our traditional values rooted in our Christian heritage.

Shortly after 9/11 our church began a series of mission trips to the Czech Republic. This nation had been under the control of atheistic communism ever since WW II, until eastern Europe, with the support of the USA, began to stand up against the Soviets. It was amazing to see the emptiness in the expressions of people after living so long under the oppression of a cold atheistic dictatorship.

I am deeply concerned that we see an increasing drift within our nation in the same direction. People have an inherent need for spiritual bread just as we need physical nourishment, if our bodies are to thrive and function as God intended. People need spiritual bread, and Jesus made it clear He is this bread. Now this statement clearly implies the next truth.

2. THE BREAD OF LIFE SAVES THE SOUL

The Bible clearly teaches that people, in our natural state as sinners, are spiritually dead and separated from God. When I say that this Bread saves, I mean it saves us from eternal death. The Bible clearly teaches that in the beginning, God created Adam and Eve in a state of innocence. But when they allowed the evil one to deceive them with his lies, they were driven out of the garden with a sentence of eternal death. The Bible clearly teaches that the payment for sin is death (Romans 6:23). If we remain spiritually dead beyond physical death, we have no hope. This is what the Bible calls the second death, which includes physical as well as spiritual death in the place called Hell.

But Jesus, as The Great I Am and The Bread of Life, having conquered the power of sin and death, has the power to quicken our souls and give new life that is everlasting. Through faith in Christ, we receive

Bread that raises us up to experience a new life, now and forevermore, even after physical death. In John 6:27, Jesus clarified the nature of this Bread when he said, "Do not labor for the food that perishes, but for food that endures to eternal life, which the Son of Man will give to you. For on Him God the Father has set His seal."

But in verses 32-35, Jesus takes it to another level: "Jesus then said to them, "Truly, truly, I say to you, it was not Moses who gave you the bread from heaven, but my Father gives you the true bread from heaven. For the bread of God is he who comes down from heaven and gives life to the world." They said to him, "Sir, give us this bread always." Jesus said to them, "I am the bread of life; whoever comes to me shall not hunger, and whoever believes in me shall never thirst."

Notice the emphasis on life. When Jesus speaks of life, He means far more than being conscious, but He is talking about a new quality of life which includes both our temporal lives while on earth, but also eternal life in heaven. Jesus describes this bread in verses 47-48, "Truly, truly, I say to you, whoever believes has eternal life. I am the bread of life". Notice that this verse is in the present tense. The moment a person believes, Jesus says they have eternal life. This means that when Jesus speaks of eternal life, He is also referring to both a quantity and quality of life.

But how can Jesus can do this? What qualifies Him to be the Bread of Life? Well, we have already learned that He is qualified because of Who He is, but a second reason is because of what He has accomplished. Notice in Verse 51 the phrase "my flesh". This is clearly a reference to the cross. He, as the great I Am, came to this world in flesh (the Incarnation) to serve as our representative to pay the penalty for our sin. He voluntarily chose to obey the Father's plan. God's precious Son willingly submitted to terrible abuse emotionally and physically as our substitute, taking upon Himself the judgment we deserve.

31

After having suffered horrendously, Jesus said "It is finished!" In the original Greek text, it is one word: Tetelestai. This word was used commonly in the first century in a couple of interesting ways. It was used as a commercial term which means, "It is paid; the debt is paid." This term was also used as a legal term. Another common practice in the first century was to prepare what was called a "Certificate of Debt". If a man was found guilty of breaking the law and sentenced to prison, an itemized list was prepared with each infraction and its corresponding penalty. After the prisoner was taken to his cell, an actual "certificate of debt" was nailed to his cell door. When the man had served his time, the "certificate of debt" was taken down with the words "paid in full" written across. He was free to go. But the Greek word would have been "tetelestai", which means It is finished or the debt has been fully paid. This is what Jesus has done for us! He has willingly come to this earth as a perfect human being and voluntarily went to the cross to experience a horrible, brutal execution as our substitute.

The reality is this, as the Evangelism Explosion gospel presentation says, "God is merciful and therefore does not want to punish us, but He is also just, and therefore must punish sin." This is what happened on the cross. But if Christ would have died never to be heard from again, then it would have discredited all that He said or claimed about Himself and his mission. But His resurrection was confirmation of all that He taught.

Now in John 6:53-58, Jesus taught some truths that shocked His listeners. In verses 53,57-58, Jesus said, "Truly, truly, I say to you, unless you eat the flesh of the Son of Man and drink his blood, you have no life in you...as the living Father sent me, and I live because of the Father, so whoever feeds on me, he also will live because of me, This is the bread that comes down from heaven, not like the bread the fathers ate and died. Whoever feeds on this bread will live forever."

Obviously, Jesus was not teaching a form of literal cannibalism. He was saying we must receive Him, and what He accomplished for us on the cross, as our only true source of eternal life and spiritual nourishment. The Lord's Supper is a beautiful symbol of this glorious truth and serves as an ongoing reminder to what extent our Father in Heaven and His beloved Son were willing to go to save sinners like you and me. Now as we partake of this Bread of Life, let us consider another wonderful truth.

3. THE BREAD OF LIFE SATISFIES THE SOUL.

Notice again what Jesus said in John 6:35, "…I am the bread of life; whoever comes to me shall not hunger, and whoever believes in me shall never thirst."

Jesus makes another astounding claim that He not only can save our souls from everlasting darkness and torment, but He can also satisfy the longings and the needs of our soul. He can completely fill the emptiness of our aching hearts.

After completing my studies in seminary. I pastored a new church plant about 15 miles from where my mother-in-law lived. Mrs. Everidge was a great cook, and so, on many Sundays after the morning service, our young family would go there for lunch. I would be so hungry and tired. But after eating one of her great meals, I would sit back, feeling totally satisfied, contented, and often drifting off for a little nap. How awful to be hungry and then eat, but never find satisfaction nor contentment.

But this is true of many people when it comes to their hungry souls. We were created with an innate need not only for physical food and water, but this is also true spiritually regarding our souls. We have an innate spiritual need that can only be satisfied by our Lord's Living Water (John 4:10-14) and His Bread of Life. David Jeremiah has written, "As the Bread of Life, Christ is the spiritual food that gives us life, sustains us, and satisfies us. We partake of His spiritual

33

nourishment when we come to Him, believe in Him, and receive Him as Savior. He satisfies our hungry heart."

Many people turn to worldly sources for the satisfaction of this inner hunger and thirst, but the temporal world has nothing to offer that satisfies these deeper yearnings. I have spent my entire adult life as a minister of the Gospel devoted to telling people that only Jesus can meet the needs of the human soul. The scriptures tell us that "all have sinned and come short of the glory of God" (Romans 3:23). People have an innate spirit of rebellion against God and the truth of His Word. But the God of this universe continues to pursue people and His Spirit convicts them and draws them to Christ. How glorious it is to offer this Bread of Life, and see empty hungry people respond with genuine repentance and faith, resulting in a transformation in their lives.

Perhaps some who are reading these words are familiar with the conversion of Charles Colson, who was criminally charged in the Watergate scandal, which ultimately led to the resignation of President Nixon. Colson was a brilliant lawyer but was willing to participate in the cover up of the administration's wrongdoing. He was once known as Nixon's "hatchet man". He was convicted and spent seven months in prison.

But prior to his sentence, an evangelical businessman introduced Colson to Jesus, and he trusted in Jesus as his Lord and Savior. His life was radically transformed. He wrote a bestselling book titled "Born Again" in which he told of his conversion and his time in prison. He started a non-profit ministry called Prison Fellowship which would grow into an international ministry to prisoners. He was also a very effective speaker; the author of more than 30 books; the host of a very popular radio program, and on I could go. The point is that this man, who was once so hungry for political power, found in it no satisfaction, but then he met Jesus and tasted the Bread of Life. The result was a transformed man whom God used to introduce thousands, possibly even millions, to Jesus as the Lord and Savior, until he passed into glory in 2012 at the age of 81.

Colson described how addictive power can be, but the experience of the Watergate scandal shocked him into the necessity of looking at the emptiness of his soul. But that emptiness was filled up when he trusted in Christ and found a satisfaction that exceeded anything he had ever imagined. How about you?

4. THE BREAD OF LIFE SUSTAINS THE SOUL.

As food strengthens and sustains our physical bodies, likewise Christ infuses strength and sustenance into our souls. He is our continual source of spiritual nourishment that sustains us from within. This informs us that we must continue day by day to feed upon the Bread of Life; not out of fear that we might possibly lose the life He has given us, but to nourish this new life and enjoy its benefits.

I made references earlier to the Old Testament story in the book of Exodus of how God miraculously provided "manna" (or bread) as nourishment for Moses and the Hebrew people after their escape from Egyptian bondage. In what manner did God make this provision available for His people? They would gather the manna daily. Each morning the people would gather from the ground this manna that looked like wafers made of coriander seed and tasted like honey. If the people tried to save some for the next day, it would spoil and grow foul. The exception for this was the Sabbath. On the day before the Sabbath, God provided twice as much manna which the people were to save for the Sabbath. The primary lesson God was teaching His people is the importance of learning to trust Him daily for His bread to sustain them. It was a tremendous lesson on faith.

Now the manna not only served to meet a practical need, but it also served as a "type". A type is an Old Testament picture that typified or prefigured certain truths about Christ revealed in the New Testament. So, manna was an Old Testament prophetic symbol which instructed believers to view Christ as our spiritual bread. Look again at John 6:32-35, "Jesus then said to them, 'Truly, truly, I say to you, it was not Moses who gave you the bread from heaven, but my Father gives you the true bread from heaven. For the bread of God is he who comes down from heaven and gives life to the world.' "They said to him", 'Sir, give us this bread always.' "Jesus said to them," 'I am the bread of life, whoever comes to me, shall not hunger, and whoever believes in me shall never thirst.'"

This reveals how important it is to maintain an ongoing relationship with Christ in order to experience the full satisfaction and strength He provides. He provides us this strength, not for living lives of selfish indulgence, but for the purpose of living lives that truly glorify the Father and the Son. This is the reason for our existence; that we will glorify our Maker and Savior.

One of the problems facing many churches today is that they are filled with weak, malnourished Christians. One of the primary ways Christ feeds and sustains us with His Bread is through Bible study. You may recall that immediately after Jesus was baptized, He was led by the Holy Spirit into the desert to be tested by the devil. This was necessary if He was going to be our Savior. The scriptures tell us that He fasted for 40 days and nights, and no doubt was experiencing intense hunger. So, Satan tried to entice Him, by saying, "If you are the Son of God, command that these stones become bread." But Christ resisted the evil one by quoting Deuteronomy 8:3, "Man shall not live by bread alone, but by every word that proceeds from the mouth of God." This was true of the two other efforts by Satan to entice Jesus to sin. Each time our Lord would respond to Satan's effort to entice Him to sin by quoting the Word of God. Now, if the perfect Son of God resisted Satan by quoting the written Word of God, how much more so should we have enough knowledge of the Holy Scriptures, so that we are equipped to resist and renounce the lies of the evil one.

Family Life published an article titled "The Scandal of Biblical Ignorance". The article drew heavily on the research of the Barna Research Group. Here are some of the shocking results: 60% of Americans cannot even name five of the Ten Commandments; fewer than half of all adults can name the four gospels; 82% of Americans believe the old saying that "God helps those who help themselves" is a verse in the Bible. Those who identified as born-again Christians did better—by one percent. Another survey of graduating high school seniors revealed that over 50 % thought that Sodom and Gomorrah were husband and wife. Another poll indicated that a considerable number of people believed that Billy Graham preached the Sermon on the Mount.

I began getting some opportunities to preach when I was a sophomore in college, and this continued periodically until I graduated. After graduating I went to seminary and while there, at the age of 23, I became a part time student pastor. After finishing seminary, I had the incredible blessing of serving as a pastor of four more churches until my retirement at the age of 68.

As the years passed, I noticed that when I referred to what I assumed was familiar Biblical passages, a lot of the congregation had no clue what I was talking about. Too many in more recent generations have a shocking ignorance of God's Word. As a result, many believers are easily confused and vulnerable to false teaching. This is because they are like infants who are malnourished. We can see that this was an issue in the church in Corinth. Notice what Paul said in I Corinthians 3:1, "But I, brothers, could not address you as spiritual people, but as people of the flesh, as infants in Christ."

Remember the words of Christ to the church at Ephesus in Revelation 3:20, "Behold, I stand at the door and knock. If anyone hears my voice and opens the door, I will come into him and eat with him, and he with me." Jesus told the church that He was knocking at the door (in a figurative sense) waiting to come in so that He could dine with them.

Jesus indicated that He wanted to break bread with them. This ought to characterize our day-to-day routine. We must make time to daily read and study the Word for spiritual nourishment.

I doubt that many of us try to get through busy days without some physical nourishment. You might get by for a short duration of time, but it would not take long before you begin to weaken and suffer mental confusion and physical exhaustion. This is also true when it comes to our spiritual well-being. In my experience, when I have allowed the demands and cares of life to overwhelm me to the point of neglecting quality time in God's Word, I begin to "grow weary in well doing". But when I take time to each day to partake of the Bread of Life through prayer, Bible reading and study, worship and fellowship, my soul is renewed and strengthened.

5. THE BREAD OF LIFE IS ALWAYS SUFFICIENT.

By this I mean that it is sufficient in its amount. There is always enough. When you turn to Christ for His bread to satisfy and sustain you, there is never a shortage. His supply is endless, and it's always more than adequate to meet your needs. Look at the experience of the Hebrews during their journey in the wilderness. Each morning they would gather the manna (the bread from heaven). When the amount of bread was measured, they always found that those who had gathered too much had nothing in excess, and those who had not gathered enough always had a sufficient amount to meet the needs of their family. In other words, the amount gathered was equal to the daily needs of each person and family.

Look again at the miraculous feeding of the 5,000 recorded in John 6. As I said earlier, this miracle was a sign or an acted-out parable, designed to teach the people a spiritual lesson. The bread that Jesus multiplied to feed the people was intended to meet a legitimate need, but it also symbolized the spiritual bread He came to share with those who struggle through life, with an even more intense hunger deep in their souls. Look at what Jesus said and did in John 6:11-13: "Jesus then took the loaves, and when he had given thanks, he distributed them to those who were seated. So also, the fish as much as they wanted. And when they had eaten their fill, He told his disciples, Gather up the fragments, that nothing may be lost." His bread is equivalent to His grace. It is always sufficient for the situation.

I have talked to alcohol and drug addicts who have turned to Christ in desperation and testify how each day the Bread of Life and His Living Water has been sufficient to satisfy and sustain them and keep them from their addictions. I have seen people face enormous crises that required help beyond themselves to get through, but the Bread of Life was sufficient to provide more than enough hope, grace, and strength to rise above the devastation and look to the future with optimism.

I have experienced this personally. You may recall that I shared in the "Introduction" to this book my spiritual journey or testimony. There is a part of my story that is still very difficult to write or talk about. I am referring to our youngest son Kevin who at the age of 32, in May of 2006, chose to commit suicide. I will not go into all the details, but I feel compelled to tell some of the story so that I can glorify my Lord's sustaining grace.

Our son Kevin was a beautiful child with a smile that could light up a room. Early on he was a happy little boy who enjoyed pestering his older brother and sister. However, at a rather young age, he began to show some obsessive-compulsive tendencies. For example, he would compulsively wash his hands over and over. He also struggled in school with classroom settings. He was tested and it was determined that he had what was called an auditory perception problem. He did not test as being slow to learn, but these other issues created problems which made him very sensitive. He struggled in grade school, but he had good teachers who were patient with him.

As he approached middle school, His mother sensed that this would be a bit overwhelming. So, she home schooled him using some excellent Christian materials. She worked with him to the point that he was able to enter and graduate from a vocational high school. He started to do a little better and worked as an assistant produce manager in two grocery chains. He married his high school sweetheart and God blessed them with a beautiful little girl. But as responsibilities grew, issues arose in their marriage, and Kevin began struggling terribly with depression and anxiety. His marriage ended after ten years. Kevin saw Christian counselors, and a psychiatrist put him on various medications.

His mother and I prayed with him and for him. We offered him our counsel and our love as best as we knew how. But he became so overwhelmed that he twice made serious attempts but miraculously survived. But then he made a third attempt, and this time he tragically succeeded.

It is difficult to find the words to express the depth of our grief. But as horrible as it was, I experienced the sufficiency of God's grace at a level unlike anything I had ever known before. The Bread of Life was more than enough to sustain me during this incredible time of emotional and physical depletion. I am not suggesting that it was easy, but the grace of God was sufficient for me.

Look again at the words of the great apostle Paul in 2 Corinthians 12:7-10, "So to keep me from becoming conceited because of the surpassing greatness of the revelations, a thorn was given me in the flesh, a messenger of Satan to harass me, to keep me from becoming conceited. Three times I pleaded with the Lord about this, that it should leave me. But he said to me, "My grace is sufficient for you, for my power is made perfect in weakness. Therefore, I will boast all the more gladly of my weaknesses, so that the power of Christ may rest upon me. For the sake of Christ, then, I am content with my weaknesses, insults, hardships, persecutions, and calamities. For when I am weak, then I am strong."

We do not know what this "thorn in the flesh" was, but one thing is clear, Paul's "thorn" was extremely painful. The Greek word translated "thorn" means a sharp stake that could be used for torturing or impaling someone. I believe that as the Spirit inspired Paul to write about his thorn with some obscurity so that believers of all ages could identify with him. No one lives on the planet without dealing with some form of pain. But for those who place their faith in Jesus, His Bread is sufficient to sustain us no matter what our source of pain may be.

6. THE BREAD OF LIFE IS RECEIVED THROUGH SIMPLE FAITH.

Faith is always the key to partaking of the blessings of God. Jesus said in Matthew 9:29, "According to your faith be it unto you." He said in Matthew 21:22, "And whatever you ask in prayer, you will receive, if you ask in faith." In fact, Jesus taught that only through believing in Him can one be saved. Consider the well-known words of Jesus in John 3:16, "For God so loved the world, that He gave his only Son, that whoever believes in Him should not perish but have eternal life." The Apostle Paul said, "For we walk by faith, not by sight." (2 Corinthians 5:7). Power is not in faith itself, but power depends on the object of our faith. Suppose I am driving in a remote area with which I am not familiar, and I come upon an old, covered bridge made of wood. What seems like the most reasonable thing to do? To inspect how much faith I have, or to first, examine the bridge itself? If the bridge is obviously weak and unstable, then I would not trust it enough to attempt to drive across. You see, the power we experience is no greater than the object in which we place our faith.

I read an illustration that stuck with me, but I am not sure of the source. Someone said that faith is like the electrical cord that comes with an appliance. The cord is the means to connect to the power that makes the appliance work. If you plug the cord into your mouth, you will not only look stupid, but your refrigerator will not cool, or your toaster will not toast. But if you plug the cord into an electrical outlet connected to a source of power, powerful things happen.

Let's once again read the words of Jesus in John 6:28-29, "Then they said to him, 'What must we do, to be doing the works of God?'" Jesus answered them, "This is the work of God that you believe in him, whom He has sent." Look at what He later says in the same conversation in John 6:35, "Jesus said to them, 'I am the bread of life; whoever comes to me, shall not hunger, and whoever believes in me shall never thirst.'" Let's also see what He also says later to the same crowd in verses 47-48, 63-64; "Truly, truly, I say to you, whoever believes in me has eternal life. I am the bread of life....it is the Spirit who gives life; the flesh is no help at all. The words that I have spoken to you are spirit and life. But there are some of you who do not believe."

The Greek word translated "believe" literally means to completely trust. It means to trust the Lord to the point that one is willing to take a leap of faith. The Spirit convicts us and convinces us to make a full commitment to Christ, and we choose to abandon all else and act upon His word. In one sense we exercise this kind of faith every day. When you eat at a restaurant, or get on an airplane, or take medication prescribed by a doctor, or get married; these are all decisions that require tremendous faith. To make these kinds of decisions requires faith in the cooks and managers at the restaurant; or faith in the pilots and mechanics, as well as the company who built the airplane; or faith in the doctor who prescribed the medication as well as faith in the pharmacist who filled the prescription. In time a person finds out for certain if the object of his or her faith was worthy of such trust.

Another level of this faith commitment is seen in marriage vows. This kind of commitment impacts your whole life and future in a very personal way. In fact, the New Testament teachings of both Christ and Paul, compares the relationship between Christ and the church to that of a bridegroom and bride. One truth is certainly clear, Jesus is faithful always to those who have become a part of His bride.

So, those who truly place their faith in Christ, and partake of His bread, discover that their faith in Him is never misplaced. I love Psalm 34:8, "Oh, taste and see that the Lord is good, Blessed is the man who trusts in Him."

I recall a man who was a new member of a church I pastored in Perrysburg, Ohio. Shortly after he joined the church, he was in a severe auto accident, and he suffered multiple serious injuries. I went to visit him in the hospital to offer support and prayers. But I think I was more blessed than he was after my visit. He was in severe intense pain, but he expressed a tremendous joy in the Lord. He kept saying, "I'm trusting in the Lord. He is my strength and refuge." He would get a little too excited sometimes, and wince with pain. During his time of recovery, He prayed, he worshiped, he witnessed, he read and meditated upon the Word. He feasted upon the Bread of Life. He inspired all of us who reached out to him, including the nurses and attendants.

7. THE BREAD OF LIFE MUST BE SHARED.

Keep in mind that Jesus began to make the claim that He was the Bread of Life shortly after He fed the five thousand. Look again at John 6:11, "Jesus then took the loaves, and when he had given thanks, he distributed them to those who were seated. So also, the fish, as much as they wanted." People were hungry, and so Jesus took a boy's lunch and performed an incredible miracle. He took the boy's five loaves and two fish and asked the disciples to instruct the people to sit down, which they all did. After Jesus gave thanks, He began to distribute the bread and fish to the disciples who in turn were to distribute food to the mass of hungry people. As they did, the bread and fish began to multiply, and the entire mass of people ate until they were all satisfied.

As we reflect upon this incredible story, I want to especially point out that as Christ performed this miracle of provision, how did He distribute the abundant supply of bread and fish to the hungry crowd? Well, Matthew, Mark, and Luke, all tell us what John implies, and this is that Jesus broke the loaves, then gave them to the disciples to distribute to the people. And Jesus is using the same strategy today. The miracle of the cross and the resurrection is called the gospel which literally means "good news", and this good news is, by its very nature, meant to be shared with people who are starving to death spiritually. The bread that Jesus offers is eternal life, and we who have received this Bread are commissioned to share it with a spiritually starved world.

There is a great historical event recorded in the Old Testament book 2 Kings 7, which illustrates this point perfectly. The city of Samaria of the northern kingdom called Israel, was suffering a terrible famine. The reason for this was that the city was under a terrible siege by the Syrian Army camped outside the city walls. The people were starving to the point of desperation. Four lepers, who were social outcasts, sat at the city gate and began to reason among themselves about their desperate plight. They said to one another, "Why are we sitting here until we die? If we say, 'let us enter the city, 'the famine is in the city, and we shall die there. And if sit we here, we will die also." (2 Kings 7:3b-4).

So, they decided to go out to the Syrian camp with the hope that they would be captured rather than executed. Can you picture in your mind these four lepers slowly approaching the Syrian camp in fear and trembling? No doubt their eyes were big as every little sound terrified them! But as they arrived just outside the camp, they heard no sound, nor did they encounter any threat. So, as they cautiously entered the camp, they could not believe their eyes. There was not a Syrian in sight.

What had happened? Yahweh, the great God of Israel, had caused the Syrians to hear the thunderous sound of speeding chariots and galloping horses. It had sounded as if a great army was approaching. The Syrians cried out to one another, "The King of Israel has hired the Hittites and Egyptians to attack us!" Panic followed, and the Syrians fled leaving all their supplies behind, including food. Well, the lepers gorged themselves as they entered the first tent and observed the massive supply. They ate and drank, and carried off silver and gold and clothing, and went and hid them. Then they came back and entered another tent, and carried off more supplies and hid them as well.

They were no doubt having a great time. But let's read what happened next in 2 Kings 7:9, "Then they said to one another, 'We are not doing right. This day is a day of good news. If we are silent and wait until morning light, punishment will overtake us; come let us go and tell the king's household." So, they made their way back to the city and informed the gatekeepers of their wonderful discovery, who then in turn informed the king. Eventually the entire city came out and plundered the camp which enabled them to survive and even thrive.

I share this Old Testament story primarily to focus on the four lepers who discovered a tremendous supply of food when not only were they starving, but so were all their fellow citizens of the city of Samaria. At first, they were so busy feeding themselves, and rejoicing over the wonderful blessing God had provided, they had forgotten about their fellow citizens. I love what the lepers said among themselves, "We are not doing right! This is a day of good news! We cannot wait any longer or some judgment will come upon us. So, let us go tell the King."

Oh, hear me my friends! We were famished spiritually until someone cared enough for us to share the good news about the unlimited supply of the Bread of Life. It is not good for us to keep this Good

News to ourselves, when there is so many people suffering from spiritual starvation.

Well, in closing this chapter, I want to once again appeal to all believers who read these words, to make sure to plan to set aside time each day to feed upon the Bread of Life through prayer and reading the Bible. I Timothy 4:6 talks about being "nourished in the words of faith and good doctrine."

David Jeremiah relates the story of an evangelist named Leland Wang who many years ago had trouble keeping a regular schedule for daily devotions. His goal was to rise early each morning to read his Bible and spend meaningful time with God. But too often he yielded to the temptation of sleeping just a little longer and would end up rushing to get ready to fulfill his morning commitments. So, he made a rule for himself: "No Bible, no breakfast." This became his motto, and he lived by it for more than 44 years, and for a while the motto spread far and wide. Many Christians adopted it as their own.

I am not suggesting that this plan should legalistically be practiced by every committed Christian. Some people have health issues or work schedules that require a different approach, but every serious follower of Jesus needs to be nourished by the Word. As David Jeremiah has written, "Spending time with the Living Word of God (Jesus) and the Written Word of God (the Bible) is necessary nourishment."

Three

"I Am the Light of the World"

John 8:1-20; 9:1-5

Key verses: John 8:12, "Again Jesus spoke to them, saying, 'I am the light of the world. Whoever follows me will not walk in darkness but will have the light of life.'"

John 9:4-5, "We must work the works of him who sent me while it is day; night is coming, when no man can work. As long as I am in the world, I am the light of the world."

Have you ever stumbled around in a dark room trying to find the light switch? Maybe you banged your shin or knocked over a lamp, but finally you managed to turn on the light. What a difference it makes when there is light!

Light is one of God's most fascinating qualities and creations. In one sense, light is inherent to the very nature of God. When God would manifest His visible glory in the Tabernacle or the Temple, a brilliant light was overwhelming. This was also true when earlier He led them through the wilderness with a pillar of fire. Whatever the setting was, God would provide a luminous cloud or smoke to help shield the eyes of the people.

You may recall that when God spoke to Moses in a shepherd's field to reveal His name as I AM or Yahweh, He did so through a bright burning bush. So, for Jesus to say, "I am the Light of the World", was a double claim to be God. First, the "I Am" phrase, and secondly, the word "light" were directly synonymous with God Himself. In the Old Testament, especially in the Psalms, we find this as an often-stated reality. Let's consider some examples: "The Lord is my light and my salvation." (Psalm 27:10); "In your light do we see light." (Psalm 36:9); "Send out your light and truth: Let them lead me." (Psalm 43:3); "The Lord will be your everlasting light." (Isaiah 60:19); "When I sit in darkness, the Lord will be a light to me." (Micah 7:5).

The Apostle John who wrote the Gospel of John would later write in 1 John 1:5, "God is light and in Him there is no darkness at all." Revelation 21:23 says of New Jerusalem, "The Lamb is it's light". So, this is saying that the source of light that will illuminate all of heaven will be the risen, glorified Jesus sitting enthroned as the King of Kings. But to quote David Jeremiah, "the light that emits from the eternal Christ isn't just physical. It's spiritual, moral, and emotional."

It is not a coincidence that prior to our Lord's claim, that He is the Light of the World, John relates the story of the woman caught in the act of adultery (John 8:1-11). The brilliance of God's holiness shined through Christ's ministry, and wherever He traveled the purity of His character exposed both the outward sins of the flesh such as adultery as well as the inward sins of arrogance and pride which produced hypocrisy. Wherever Jesus traveled, His light revealed human wickedness. But His light also brought gracious forgiveness and hope (John 8:10-12).

How does this glorious truth apply to our lives today? What impact does the Light of Christ have in our current times?

THE INWARD EFFECT OF THE LIGHT OF THE WORLD

Notice again the promise Jesus made in John 3:12b, "…Whoever follows me will not walk in darkness but will have the light of life." Therefore, Jesus makes a profound statement with this promise. When we open up our souls to the light of Christ through a personal commitment to follow Him, His radiant presence becomes a light within our souls. The scriptures clearly teach that in our natural state as sinners we live in spiritual darkness. Due to original sin, as well as our conscious choices to sin, we are all guilty before a Holy God.

But Christ, the Son of God, came to this fallen world to dispel the darkness by living a perfect life and ultimately going to the cross, as our representative, and taking upon Himself the judgment we deserve. He died a horrific death on a cruel Roman cross, but rose again on the third day in a glorious resurrected body, as a confirmation that the powers of darkness will not ultimately prevail. He went through all the darkness of sin's curse, so that we might experience the breaking through of the glorious radiance of God's light into our souls.

I love the description of the famous Methodist missionary E. Stanley Jones who said: "When I met Christ, I felt that I had swallowed sunshine." This inward effect of the light of Christ breaks through like the sunlight pierces the early morning darkness. Notice that Jesus says that His light is experienced by those who follow Him. It is an ongoing experience as we day by day choose to walk in intimate communion with Christ. But how does this daily walk in the light of Christ affect us inwardly?

1. HIS LIGHT ILLUMINATES THE MIND.

His Light penetrates our intellect with truth. A study of the Bible reveals that light is often used as a metaphor for truth. But in our natural state as sinners, our minds are darkened by lies and deception, and so we are not able to perceive spiritual truth. Look at what the Apostle Paul wrote in 1 Corinthians 2:14,"The natural man does not accept the things of the Spirit of God, for they are folly to him, and he is not able to understand them because they are spiritually discerned." Let's also look at Paul's amazing words inspired by the Holy Spirit in 2 Corinthians 4:3-4,"and even if our gospel is veiled, it is veiled to those who are perishing. In their case the god of this world has blinded the minds of the unbelievers, to keep them from seeing the light of the gospel of the glory of Christ, who is the image of God."

Satan tries to take advantage of people who have never been enlightened by the gospel. He attempts to blind them to the truth with various lies and deception. But in the glorious light of Christ our minds come to a knowledge of truth. The Spirit of God helps us find the missing pieces to the puzzle of life. I plead with skeptics who may be reading this book, to not allow yourself to be deceived by the lies of Satan and the doubts that other skeptics may try to feed into your minds. Be open to the Gospel truth.

Christianity does not call for a blind leap into the darkness of ignorance and fairy tales, wishing that it were all true. One little boy was asked to define faith. He responded by saying, "faith is believing something that ain't true". It's amazing how many people agree with him. But the Christian faith is based on an historical documented revelation of truth. In Jesus Christ, God the Light came to this earth to illuminate our minds with His Truth. And the primary way He does this is through His Spirit and His Word. As we study the written Word of God, The Holy Spirit of God Illuminates our minds through giving us an understanding of what we have read or heard.

The Spirit accomplishes this first, THROUGH HIS ABSOLUTE TRUTH.

The word absolute means ultimate, complete, unconditional, and unqualified. It is fixed and non-negotiable. It doesn't change when circumstances change. Truth is not relative, depending on the situation. Absolute truth is objective, universal and constant.

Jesus is the Light whether an individual ever personally encounters Him or not. He always has been, and He always will be. And His light is not off and on like a flashing neon sign. He isn't sometimes light and sometimes darkness.

One of the tragedies of today's culture is the rejection of the belief in absolute truth. Relativism has taken over in our institutions of higher learning; in our political persuasions and operations; in our entertainment industry; and sadly, even in our mainline Protestant denominations as well as some of our evangelical ministries. Many today define for themselves what they want truth to be, rather than what it is, based on the revelation which our Creator has given to us in the Holy Scriptures. In our modern culture, this so called "truth" depends on our human circumstances, feelings and desires.

The acceptance and practice of abortion is a powerful example of how far our society has declined. People can more easily justify ending a human life prior to birth if they can accept that there is no absolute moral and spiritual truth by which we will be judged. This also applies to other contemporary issues such as same sex marriage, transgender issues, and on I could go. My purpose is not to condemn people who engage in such sinful practices, for the Bible clearly teaches that all of us have sinned and fall short of the glory of God. But the point is that our Creator has given us some absolute moral truths by which we must live, and if we disregard these absolutes, we do so at our own peril. It does not matter what is popular or culturally acceptable or "woke", but what does matter is what God says. And what God says determines what is right and wrong. Right is right even if nobody is right, and wrong is wrong even if everybody is wrong.

The Light of Jesus is absolute truth even when it comes to our eternal salvation. Later we will look at another "I Am" saying of Jesus, which focuses on this great truth, but I do want to briefly introduce it now. Look at John 14:6 where Jesus says the following to Thomas, "I am the way and the truth and the life. No one comes to the Father except through me." This is stated as an absolute truth. Jesus did not say I am a way or an alternative way, He clearly said I am the one and only way to God the Father in heaven.

Jesus is also absolute truth when it comes to making moral choices in everyday living. The Lord of light has given us principles and precepts by which we are to live our lives. We find these in the scriptures. For example, Psalm 119:11 says, "Your word I have hidden in my heart, that I might not sin against You". Let us not forget that the Bible is described as the written word of God inspired by the Holy Spirit. In John chapter one Jesus is called the Word of God clothed in flesh. Look at John 1:14, "And the Word became flesh and dwelt among us, and we have seen His glory, glory as of the only Son from the Father, full of grace and truth"

This leads to a second way His Spirit illuminates our minds, and this is THROUGH HIS APPLIED TRUTH.

His Light gives our minds knowledge and understanding that has practical application. I mentioned earlier in this chapter the importance of principles and precepts. But what do these terms mean? I am not sure where I got these definitions but here they are: A PRINCIPLE is a rule or standard that may be applied to more than one situation; A PRECEPT is a command or law that is very specific in nature. You can find principles and precepts throughout scriptures which were all inspired by the Holy Spirit.

So, as we follow the light of Christ, His Spirit who indwells us will take His absolute truth and apply it in practical ways to our lives. In other words, He takes the light of His objective truth and begins to focus it like a laser beam on some situation in our lives and it becomes very subjective or personal. It becomes applied truth.

I can recall numerous times in my life when I have been reading, studying or listening to someone teaching the Bible, and suddenly the indwelling Spirit of Jesus began to take His truth found in Scripture and make it very personal and applicable to my life situation. It's as if a light was turned on in my mind. But not only does His light illuminate the mind, but a second reality is the impact His light has on our hearts.

2. HIS LIGHT TRANSFORMS THE HUMAN HEART

In the Bible the word "heart" refers to the place where one's character develops. It is the seat of our affections, attitudes and motivations. In our Lord's Sermon on the Mount beginning in Matthew 5, He introduces His message by listing what has been traditionally called the Beatitudes. Each Beatitude begins with the phrase "Blessed are…" followed by some character quality and then closes with a specific promised blessing. The sixth Beatitude says, "Blessed are the pure in heart, for they shall see God".

But because of sin we all have a heart problem. Due to original sin, we all have a natural inclination to sin.

However, through the Light of Christ the human heart can be changed or transformed. How does the Light of the World do this.

First, THE LIGHT OF CHRIST EXPOSES OUR HEARTS.

This is true of all forms of light. It exposes whatever is covered by the darkness. I remember as a boy exploring a small, wooded area not very far behind our home. I saw an old log and out of curiosity flipped it over. And suddenly as the sunlight burst forth upon all the little bugs hiding under this old piece of wood, they started scattering in every direction. I am certain that if these little creatures could have communicated with me, they would have been screaming at me; why don't you leave us alone? They were comfortable in their little world of darkness.

Of course, the brighter the sunlight, the more visible and obvious everything becomes. Flaws, blemishes, or dirty spots may not be that noticeable in a dimly lit room, but they are all very observable out in the bright sunlight. I recall one time dropping some mustard and other assorted things on a white shirt I was wearing, so I wiped it off and it looked okay to me. But when I went out into bright sunlight and looked down, I discovered that I looked like a walking McDonald's hamburger. The light exposed me.

We may somewhat successfully hide from others what is in our hearts, but the Light of Christ shines all the way into our feelings, motivations and hidden sins. Our sinful heart condition blends in with the darkness of a fallen world, but the brightness of Christ's light is in sharp contrast. This is why the world tried to put out the light of Christ. His light disturbs us, convicts us, makes us feel uncomfortable. It's like the little bugs that seemed very disturbed when I kicked over the log and exposed them to the brilliant sunlight. The Bible says that men love darkness rather than light. But if we submit to the glorious light of Christ, something wonderful happens! For not only does the Light of the World expose us, but he also purifies us.

Second, THE LIGHT OF CHRIST PURIFIES OUR HEARTS

In the Bible, light not only symbolizes truth, but it also represents the purity or holiness of God. When the light of Christ exposes our sin, and we confess and repent of our sin, followed by a yielding to His light, He begins to cleanse and purify our hearts. Then the third person of the Trinity, the Holy Spirit, continues to make us Holy as He is Holy. This is called sanctification.

The light of Christ works like a spiritual laser light. I read that light travels as straight lines in waves. With laser light all the light waves are the same length, and the crests of the waves are all lined up. This enables the light to be focused with tremendous power on a very small spot. It is common knowledge today that lasers are often used to perform certain types of surgeries. So, likewise the Holy Light of Christ is focused on the hearts of those who come to Him in faith. His intense and penetrating Holiness burns and cuts away the impurities within our souls and with great love He begins to change us inside out.

And as His light does this…

Third, THE LIGHT OF CHRIST ENERGIZES OUR HEARTS

We all know that light waves carry energy. In fact, we could not survive physically on this planet without light. Notice the phrase Jesus uses in verse 12, "I am the light of the world. Whoever follows me will not walk in darkness but will have the light of light." When the world tried to put out the light of Christ, it failed. He arose from the dead! And friend, if you have never opened your heart to the Light of the World, you are choosing ultimately an eternal destiny of utter darkness separated from God who is the source of all that is good, beautiful and meaningful. This begins even in this life for those who choose not to open their hearts up to the Light of Jesus.

The Apostle Paul wrote in 2 Corinthians 5:17, "Therefore, if anyone is in Christ, he is a new creation. The old has passed away; behold , the new has come." So, when we open our hearts to the light of Christ, He will give us new life. He will spiritually energize our souls with the literal indwelling of His Holy Spirit. As He purifies us, He transforms us inside out with a new power to live differently. This does not mean that we become perfect in our everyday life, but the indwelling light of Christ will lovingly but sometimes painfully, focus like a laser on things in our lives that need to be burned off. He then energizes us with new hope and motivation to become more conformed to the image of Christ even in this life.

Josh McDowell is one of the great Christian apologists of my generation. His first book was titled "More than a Carpenter". The book is basically his testimony of how Christ transformed him from a skeptic to a passionate believer in the Gospel. One of the remarkable events he writes about is the transformation of his relationship with his dad. Prior to his conversion, his heart was filled with hatred for his alcoholic father. It was glaring and ugly. But after he received Christ, the Light of Christ exposed to Josh how awful and displeasing this hatred was before Holy God. Josh humbled himself, and confessed his sin in a spirit of genuine repentance.

The result was miraculous. The Light of Christ did an amazing thing in the heart of Josh. His heart was purified. He not only forgave his father, but the light of Christ transformed his cold heart into one that was filled with compassion toward this man he at one time despised. The result is that the Light of Christ energized Josh to be reconciled to his father and later he would lead his father to a personal commitment of his life to Christ. Indeed, the Light of Christ does transform human hearts.

3. THE LIGHT OF CHRIST GUIDES OUR WILLS.

So far, we have focused first, on how the Light of the World illuminates the mind by penetrating the intellect with His truth, but then secondly; we looked at how His Light transforms the heart which is the seat of our attitudes, motivations and passions. Now a third effect of the Light of the World is that He serves as a guiding light for the human will. Notice in verse 12 that after Jesus declares, "I am the Light of the World", He immediately declares, "Whoever follows me will not walk in darkness". So, the words "follow" and "walk" clearly imply acts of the will. Christ has come to be our guiding light as we travel the path of life in this world of spiritual darkness.

In my introduction, I mentioned the impact that my grandma Jones had upon me spiritually. She and my uncle Clark lived on a small farm about five miles south of London, Kentucky. It was there that they operated a little country grocery store, and as a small child I loved to visit there except for one thing. Back in the early fifties, they did not have an indoor toilet. And so, to go "to the bathroom", you had to walk down this little path to what was called the "outhouse". In my mind, I was convinced that at nighttime her little farm had to be the darkest spot on the face of the earth. You could hear strange noises made by all kinds of little creatures. But my grandma Jones had this big ole flashlight which was always available for me to use if needed. So, if I needed to go during the night, I would turn that "baby" on and follow the light of my flashlight which showed me the path (to relief).

This is another important function of light in that it provides guidance when one is trying to walk down a dark path. The Magi followed a bright star until it led them to the Christ child. Likewise, Jesus, the Light of the World, will always lead us down the right path if we willfully choose to follow Him.

Consider with me three ways His Light guides our wills:

First, HE PROVIDES PERCEPTION.

As we journey through life, we are constantly confronted with choices. Some choices are very insignificant, such as the color of socks we choose to wear each day. But other decisions are of great significance and have great consequences dependent on what choices we make. To make the right decisions, our human wills need the perception that only the light of Christ can provide. Through His Word and His Spirit, Jesus provides insight and discernment. His Light gives us perspective and points of orientation.

As a young adult I began to be fascinated by lighthouses. This began to grow especially after I was called to pastor the First Baptist Church in Perrysburg, Ohio which is basically a suburb of Toledo. Being in northwestern Ohio placed us closer to Lake Erie. We discovered that we were about 50 miles from a beautiful little community with a "cool" lighthouse right on the edge of Lake Erie. This community is named Marblehead, and it became a getaway place for Brenda and me. Even after I was called to pastor Dublin Baptist, which was in a suburb of Columbus, we would still occasionally go to the area for a day. Sometimes our vacations would involve looking for lighthouses.

Now, some may be curious about my fascination with lighthouses. Aside from the beauty of their locations, the primary interest began to develop in my heart because for me personally, a lighthouse became a powerful reminder that Jesus is the Light of the World. A lighthouse is stationed near a body of water. Its primary purpose is to provide those who are traveling on the sea, a point of orientation. Especially in times of utter darkness or raging storms, if those directing the ship can see the lighthouse it gives them perspective and clarity in steering the ship. And likewise, this is true for us in our relationship with Jesus.

Even in times of great distress and darkness, if we keep our eyes firmly fixed on Jesus, He will give us the light and perception we need to make the right choices. But He not only provides perception—

Second, HE PROVIDES PURPOSE

Way back in 1965 the Beatles released a song called "Nowhere Man". The first lines of the song say, "He's a real nowhere man, sitting in his nowhere land, making all his nowhere plans for nobody. Doesn't have a point of view, knows not where He's going to....He's as blind as he can be, just sees what he wants to see". There is a rumor that John Lennon wrote the song about himself during a time of discouragement.

I don't know how accurate the rumor is, but it certainly describes the lives of millions of people in the world today. Another line in the song "Doesn't have a point of view, knows not where he's going to". There is another unsubstantiated rumor that not long before he was assassinated, John had made a personal commitment to Christ. Others have questioned this, or said that if he did, it did not last long. Steve Turner wrote an article in Christianity Today, June 12, 2000, on what some described as a short-term conversion. Of course, only God knows the human heart. But this is the problem facing millions of souls in today's world. All around us we encounter "Nowhere people" living lives without clarity or meaning. They have no overarching purpose that gives them hope for the future.

But those who have truly committed their lives to Jesus Christ are driven by a very clear purpose. Those who follow the light of Jesus are on an indescribable journey. His light leads us to a glorious destiny called heaven. As He guides us His light gives us direction and meaning to our journey of hope, for both in this life and for the life to come. Our ultimate destiny is "the new heaven and the new earth" totally purged from all the effects of sin.

His light also leads to tremendous meaning and significance even on the earth. He provides perfect direction for this life and the life to come. He has a unique purpose for each of our lives as we continue to follow His light. I think of the Lord's call of Jeremiah described in Jeremiah 1:4-10 (read this and meditate on what it meant then and what it means today).

Third, HE PROVIDES PERSONAL LEADERSHIP.

Look again at the word "follow" in verse 12 where Jesus says, "I am the light of the world. Whoever follows me will not walk in darkness but will have the light of life." What an incredible statement! The secret to finding guidance from Yahweh is to follow His one and only Son, Jesus, the Light of the World. The Greek word translated "follow" implies faithfulness, obedience, discipleship, and companionship. Jesus literally offers His personal leadership and says, "follow me! Walk with me! Lean on me! Put me first in your life, and I will teach you incredible truth and empower you to live a life of eternal significance." All our difficult decisions become much clearer when we first seek Him as the Lord of our lives. The only way through the darkness is to follow the light He gives us.

Imagine yourself in a deep dark cave following a guide who has a large flashlight. You have no idea what is ahead. Occasionally you hear strange sounds and feel little drops of water fall upon your brow. As you follow the light of the guide, you also notice that periodically there are sharp narrow turns to make, as well as different alternative paths that the guide passes by. As the journey continues a little longer than expected, you begin to wonder if the guide knows what he is doing and where he is going. But then you begin to see the sunlight peeking through, and you realize that all along the way the guide knew what he was doing and where he was going. And this is also true of Jesus, The Light of the World.

Let us look again at the context of this amazing claim. Earlier before He made this claim in verse 12, Jesus had been engaged in a dialogue with many Jews in the Temple. And this took place during one of the great annual Jewish festivals called the Feast of the Tabernacles. This feast commemorated God's provision for the Hebrew people during the wilderness wanderings.

You may recall that the Lord had guided the Hebrew people with a pillar of cloud during the day and a pillar of fire at night. Moses and the people obeyed the movement of the pillar. Where it rested, that's where they pitched their tents. And they moved on only when its movement beckoned them onward. The pillar of fire had been the evidence of the presence of God with them. He had been their light in darkness; giving them direction, hope, and courage.

To commemorate this supernatural guidance from the Lord, there was an annual ceremony at the close of the Feast of the Tabernacles called the Illumination of the Temple. It was observed each evening in the court of the Women. First, there was "the court of the Gentiles", then "the court of the women" (Israelites only), then "the court of the Israelites" (male Israelites only), and finally, "the court of the priests" who alone had access to this place where they offered sacrifices for the sins of the people.

The Illumination of the Temple was observed where four great candelabra stood in the center of the court. And then at the appointed time a very dramatic event occurred as they were set ablaze. This served as a powerful reminder of the glorious light God had been for h

His people during a terrible time of darkness and fear during the Exodus. Let us not forget that this is the location where, earlier on the same day, Jesus had been confronted by some scribes and Pharisees who had brought to Him a women caught in an act of adultery! This was orchestrated by the enemies of Jesus who wanted to expose Him because they believed He was a false messiah.

Imagine what it was like that day in the Temple when, after Jesus had showed compassion and grace for this woman caught in an act of adultery, it appears that immediately He directed His attention to the Pharisees and said, "I am the light of the world. Whoever follows me will not walk in darkness but will have the light of life." Wow!

Jesus has come to be our light, and guide us as He did the Israelites through the wilderness. Even if you have been living an ungodly life like the adulterous women, He invites you to follow Him. For He overcomes the darkness and gives light to those who choose to repent and believe. Once you make such a commitment, it calls for a moment by moment walk with Him. We must hide His words in our hearts, spend time with Him in prayer and learn to listen to the prompting of His Spirit. But the Light not only inwardly affects our lives, but also has an outward affect.

THE OUTWARD EFFECT OF THE LIGHT OF THE WORLD

When the light of Christ enters our souls and begins to change us inside out, we become lanterns through which His light shines. He has placed His light in us as His born-again followers and He has commissioned us to brightly shine for His glory. During His famous Sermon on the Mount, He even told His followers, "You are the light of the world. A city set on a hill cannot be hidden. Nor do people light a lamp and put it under a basket, but on a stand and it gives light to all in the house. In the same way, let your light shine before others, so that they may see your good works and give glory to your Father who is in heaven."(Matthew 5:13-16)

The great Apostle Paul had the same emphasis in his letters to the New Testament churches. Let's look at some examples: Romans 2:19, "... you yourself are a guide to the blind, a light to those who are in darkness"; Ephesians 5:8, "For you were once darkness, but now you are light in the Lord. Walk as children of light." In Philippians 2:15, Paul spoke of "a crooked and perverse generation among whom you shine as lights in the world."

As His light shines through us, what will happen? Consider with me four specific results of His light consistently shining in and through us:

First, HIS Light Penetrates Society.

Jesus told His followers that they must never be guilty of hiding their LIGHT. He said that typically people do not put a lantern under a basket. If light is to be of any benefit, it must be positioned to freely shine. I'm sure many who are reading these words have been to a special service during the Christmas or Easter seasons where upon entry, every person is given a small wax candle. Later at a designated time the overhead lights are significantly dimmed. Typically, the pastor talks about the importance of passing on the light of Jesus to others who live in darkness. A large candle or candelabra has been pre-lit to symbolize the presence of Christ. The pastor then lights his candle off the Christ candle. Then he begins to quickly light the candles of others. And as others do the same, in a short time the room is penetrated with light.

We who have received His light must pass it on to others who are living in spiritual darkness. This is the primary mission Christ gave to His followers before He ascended back into heaven. We must get out of our buildings and stop waiting for people to find their way to us. We have a commission from our Lord to take the gospel light to all peoples and nations.

Second, HIS Light Reveals Sin.

Notice Paul's inspired words to the Ephesians in 5:11-13, "Take no part in the unfruitful works of darkness, but instead expose them. For it is shameful to even speak of the things that they do in secret. But when anything is exposed by the light, it becomes visible, for anything that becomes visible is light. Therefore, it says, 'Awake, O sleeper, arise from the dead, and Christ will shine on you." The light of Christ in us will be a real contrast to the world, if it is not hidden. Our lifestyles, including our speech, should be like a light that God can use to convict people of their sin. Our calling is not to condemn sinners personally. We must leave that to God, but through our holy living and our stand against sin, the light of Christ can expose the ugliness and perversion of sin. We must love the sinner, but our light should also reveal sin for what it is, before our Holy God.

Third, HIS Light Attracts the Seeker.

Light attracts the attention of people. I can remember as a child always being fascinated by those high-beam searchlights shining up and moving across the night sky. They were often used to attract attention to a carnival or some special sales event at a local business. But light not only attracts attention to some special event, but it also can attract our attention because of its inherent beauty. The spectrum of colors is determined by the wavelength of light. The Old Testament story of God creating and choosing a rainbow to remind people throughout time that he would never use water to destroy the earth again, has been a powerful sign to humanity throughout the ages.

Oh dear reader, both physically and spiritually, nothing can compare to the beauty and glory of the light of Jesus. Let us not forget both the pre and post incarnate glory of God the Son. During the Old Testament times the Son of God would occasionally intervene in the affairs of Israel in bodily form. These are called by some a Christophany. The Old Testament writers would often refer to these Christophanies as the Angel of the Lord. The word "angel" means messenger. Great examples can be seen in the experiences of Hagar, Gideon and the three young Hebrew men (Shadrach, Meshach and Abednego).

After Christ died a horrible death on the cross, we know that on the third day He arose from the dead with a new glorified body. After His ascension back into heaven, He later appeared to Saul of Tarsus who was on his way to Damascus to arrest and persecute those who were preaching the gospel. Saul, who would later be known as Paul the Apostle, was overwhelmed by what he described as "a great light from heaven shining around him"(Acts 22:6). He later (Acts 26:13) describes this same experience as seeing "a light from heaven, brighter than the sun, shining around him".

This describes the Lord Jesus as He appeared to Saul of Tarsus at the time of Saul's conversion and call to be an apostle of the gospel to Jews and Gentiles. This was a unique event in the early history of the church. The primary way the light of Christ shines today is through the witness and good works of His followers. I mentioned earlier the words of Christ in Matthew 5:14-16. This is where Jesus refers to His followers as being like a bright shining city sitting on a hill for all to see, or a lampstand that gives light to an entire house.

Our primary calling as Christ followers today is obviously not to repel people from Christ. But if we are allowing the true light of Jesus to shine through us, those who are sincerely seeking spiritual truth and direction will be drawn by the Holy Spirit to the Lord Jesus Christ.

Fourth, HIS Light Liberates those who Surrender.

Let me state the obvious: What a difference it makes when you can see clearly! Let us not forget the context of this teaching by Jesus. Jesus made the statement about Himself being the Light of the World shortly after forgiving the repentant woman seized in the act of adultery. Remember what He said to this poor woman right before declaring she was free to go—John 8:10-11, "Jesus stood up and said to her, 'Woman, where are they? Has no one condemned you?' She said , 'No one, Lord' And Jesus said, 'Neither do I condemn you: go, and from now on sin no more.'"

Later in the same chapter Jesus said to some Jews who believed in Him, "and you will know the truth and the truth will set you free." (John 8:32) Then in chapter 9, look at what Jesus said before healing a man who had been blind from birth: "As long as I am in the world, I am the light of the world." He then proceeded to heal the man's eyes by enabling him to see for the first time in his life.

As Jesus gave this man his physical sight setting him free from blindness, He was also revealing the truth that He came to enable the spiritually blind to see which is an even greater miracle. This is what happens to us when we trust in Jesus alone as our Lord and Savior. As the great old hymn says, "I once was lost but now I'm found, was blind but now I see."

Jesus has not changed. He is still the Light of the World!!!!

Four

"I Am the Good Shepherd"

John 10:1-5; "Truly, truly, I say to you, he who does not enter the sheepfold by the door but climbs in by another way, that man is a thief and a robber. But he who enters by the door is the shepherd of the sheep. To him the gatekeeper opens. The sheep hear his voice, and he calls his own sheep by name and leads them out. When he has brought out all his own, he goes before them, and the sheep follow him, for they know his voice. A stranger they will not follow, but will flee from him, for they do not know the voice of strangers."

John 10:7-11; "Jesus again said to them,' Truly, truly, I say to you, I am the door of the sheep. All who come before me are thieves and robbers, but the sheep do not listen to them. I am the door. If anyone enters by me, he will be saved and will go in and out and find pasture. The thief comes only to steal and kill and destroy. I came that they might have life and have it abundantly. I am the Good Shepherd. The Good Shepherd lays down his life for the sheep.'"

John 10:14-15; "I am the Good Shepherd. I know my own and my own know me, just as the Father knows me, and I know the Father; and I lay down my life for the sheep."

I read the story about a young boy who came home from Sunday School, and his parents asked him what the lesson had been about. The boy replied, "Ah, same ole stuff; shepherds and sheep, sheep and shepherds." Well, indeed there are a lot of references to shepherds and sheep in the Bible. The Biblical writers and Jesus Himself often spoke by using the common images of their time. One of the most familiar figures in Israel was the shepherd, and so the picture of the shepherd and his sheep is woven into the language of the scriptures.

But I think that a lot of us can relate to the little boy, because the closest most people in our culture get to a shepherd is a guy acting as a shepherd in a Christmas pageant. And for many, their understanding of sheep is limited to wool clothing or the price of lamb in a meat department.

But Jesus said, "I AM the Good Shepherd", and this means that if we take Him seriously, we will take seriously the metaphor of the shepherd, which He employed to help us understand the nature of our relationship with Him as His followers. I personally believe this statement, "I AM the Good Shepherd", is one of the most beautiful and powerful descriptions Jesus gives of Himself.

So, as we continue our study of the " I Am" statements of Jesus, I want to first focus on:

1. THE GOOD SHEPHERD'S CLAIM

First, He Claimed to be God.

We have already observed earlier in this study, that the phrase "I Am" is a claim to be Yahweh God. It was His personal name which He revealed to Moses at the "Burning Bush". But when Jesus called himself "The Good Shepherd", He was using a different expression to also claim deity. Every Jew from the time he or she was a small child was taught that Yahweh (the great I AM) was the Shepherd of Israel. The Old Testament is filled with references to God being the Shepherd and His people being the flock. The most familiar passage is of course the 23rd Psalm which begins with the well-known phrase, "The Lord (Yahweh) is my Shepherd." And so, Jesus used two phrases 'I Am" and "the Good Shepherd" to describe His identity. And both phrases from the Old Testament were equated with God.

Notice that Jesus said, I am "the", not "a", Good Shepherd. He is the one and only Good Shepherd. And so, once again, we are confronted with an astounding claim. Jesus of Nazareth, clearly claimed to be the one and only Shepherd of Israel. And for Him to make such a claim was equivalent to Jesus claiming to be the one and only true God of the universe. So, this means that He is either who He claimed to be, or is deceived, or is a deceiver. The "I AM sayings" of Jesus leave no middle ground. We must either worship Him or reject Him. What is your conclusion? Now with His claim to be God, He was making another astonishing claim:

Second, He Claimed to be The Savior of God's People.

In this chapter ten of John's gospel, Jesus spoke of two kinds of sheepfolds. First, He described the sheepfolds in towns and villages which were called communal sheepfolds. This is where all the village flocks sheltered when they returned home at night. These folds were protected by a strong door to which only the shepherds held the keys. This is the kind of fold described in verses 2-3.

But when the sheep were out on the hills in the warm season, they did not necessarily return to the village at night. They were collected into sheepfolds on the hillsides. These hillside sheepfolds were just open spaces enclosed by a wall. There was just one opening by which the sheep could go in and out. And so, the opening had no actual physical door. Therefore, at night the shepherd would literally lay down across the opening and no sheep could come or go except over the shepherd's body.

In a very literal sense, the shepherd was the door. There was no access to the sheepfold except through him. Let's look again at verses 7-9, "So Jesus again said to them, "Truly, truly, I say to you, I am the door of the sheep. All who come before me are thieves and robbers, but the sheep did not listen to them. I am the door, if anyone enters by me, he will be saved and will go in and out and find pasture."

Now sheep are very dependent and dumb animals. Without a shepherd they are prone to wander off with no sense of direction. They are defenseless and vulnerable. The Bible often portrays people without God as being like sheep without a shepherd. Does this describe you? Look at what the prophet Isaiah said about the human condition: Isaiah 53:6, "All we like sheep have gone astray; we have turned—every one—to his own way".

Let's also investigate the New Testament and read the description that Matthew gives of Jesus as He ministers to the masses. Matthew 9:36, "When He saw the multitudes, he was moved with compassion for them, because they were weary and scattered like sheep having no shepherd." Does this describe you? Well, Jesus came to save you! He has come to be your shepherd, and lead you safely into His fold. And only He can do it! He is the only door! Now, another truth Jesus reveals about Himself is that because He is God and Savior, the only conclusion must be that:

Third, Jesus is indeed the Lord of Lords and King of Kings.

If Jesus is God incarnate and the Good Shepherd, then He has authority over all our lives as His sheep. We must seek to follow and obey Him as sheep follow and obey their shepherd. Notice the description that Jesus gives of the response of the sheep to their

70

shepherd in verses 3-5; "To him the gatekeeper opens. The sheep hears his voice, and he calls his own sheep by name and leads them out. When he has brought out all his own, he goes before them, and the sheep follow him, for they know his voice." Notice how Jesus emphasizes that the sheep only respond to their shepherd, and they will not follow a stranger.

Jesus warns that there will be others who will claim to be the Good Shepherd, but they are false shepherds and deceivers, who are motivated by self-interest rather than the welfare of the flock. He identifies some of these strangers as thieves and robbers. Look at what he says in verses 8 and 10. "All who came before me are thieves and robbers, but the sheep did not listen to them....the thief only comes to steal and kill and destroy. I came that they might have life and have it abundantly." The thief no doubt represents the devil and his followers who have no interest in the welfare of the Lord's flock, but his strategy is to use deception and sneak in and attack the sheep. But the Good Shepherd's goal is to enable his flock to thrive with abundant productive living.

There are others whom Jesus describes as hired hands (or hirelings). Jesus clearly implies that these hired hands only work out of self-interest, and have no sense of loyalty to the owner nor the welfare of the sheep. But on the other hand, this can also be true of owners. There are many in this fallen world who will call for our allegiance and on the surface what they offer sounds appealing, but ultimately their purpose is to use us for their gain with little concern for our future welfare. Look at the words of Jesus in verses 12-13, "He who is a hired hand and not a shepherd, who does not own the sheep, sees the wolf coming and leaves the sheep and flees, and the wolf snatches them and scatters them. He flees because he is a hired hand and cares nothing for the sheep." If we don't follow the true and good Shepherd of our souls, we will find substitutes. Another word consistently used in the Bible as a substitute for God is the word idol. The first and second commandments given to Moses cover this sin. We are commanded to not have any other god before Yahweh, nor are we to bow down in worship of any idol.

All of us by nature spiritually need to follow the Good Shepherd. That is the way God wired us. If we don't follow Jesus as the Shepherd of our souls, we will find substitutes as idols. Prior to Christ's coming to this earth, during Old Testament times, God primarily spoke through prophets, priests and kings, but when Jesus came the Apostle John was inspired by the Spirit to write that Jesus was the Word of God incarnate (John 1:1-3,14). This is why He is the true Shepherd. He calls upon us all to follow Him and obey His will. Notice in John 10:3-5, that His sheep respond only to their Shepherd, and they will not respond to the voice of a stranger.

Notice again what Jesus said in verses 11-12, "I am the good shepherd. The good shepherd lays down his life for the sheep. He who is a hired hand and not a shepherd, who does not own the sheep, sees the wolf coming and leaves the sheep and flees, and the wolf snatches them and scatters them." Oh, what a glorious truth! Jesus, our Good Shepherd, is fully committed to our care. All of us by nature spiritually need a shepherd to follow. This is the way God made us. If we don't follow the true and good Shepherd, our souls will find substitutes. To whom or to what will you commit your life? The Good Shepherd, or the devil, whom Jesus describes in verse 10 as a thief who comes to steal, kill and destroy?

This is the decision that confronts every human being. Choose whom you will serve. Will you choose to serve yourself living a life dominated by self-interest? Or will you choose to serve the Divine Shepherd whose name is Jesus, the Son of Almighty God? We were created to serve the Lord. He alone is worthy of our worship, adoration and service! If we attempt to follow idols and false gods, it will only lead to a life of emptiness and ultimately a place called hell.

I came across this poem a few years ago:

King Heroin is my shepherd, I shall always want; he maketh me to lie down in gutters, he leadeth me beside the troubled waters, he destroyed my soul.

Drug addiction is only one of many ways the thief comes to steal, and kill, and destroy. (John 10:10a)

2. THE GOOD SHEPHERD'S CARE

The 23rd Psalm (KJV) begins with the very familiar words, "The Lord is my Shepherd, I shall not want".

One little girl misquoted this verse, but she had the right idea when she said, " The Lord is my Shepherd, that's all I want." This beautiful verse literally means, "because the Lord is my shepherd, I have everything I need"; or "I lack nothing"; or "I shall want nothing". When we enter the Lord's sheepfold, just as a good shepherd is committed to care for his sheep, likewise, the Lord is committed to care for and meet the needs of His sheep. Let's consider some of the blessings that come with the Good Shepherd's care.

First, The Good Shepherd Knows His Sheep.

Note in John 10:14,27 how Jesus emphasizes His relationship with his sheep. Verse 14, "I am the good shepherd. I know my own and my own know me"; verse 27, "My sheep hear voice, and I know them, and they follow me". In Israel a real relationship developed between a shepherd and his sheep. The sheep were kept primarily for their fleece, and often sheep would remain with the same shepherd for years. The shepherds would even give names such as "brown leg" or 'black ear". And so good shepherds knew their sheep individually. Likewise, Jesus was saying to his followers I know each one of you personally. I know your name. In fact, the Greek word translated know, doesn't mean to just know about a person, but it means to know through personal knowledge. It means to know in the sense of having a personal relationship with someone.

Matthew 7:23 records Jesus saying that on the day of judgment, He will say to some; "I never knew you, depart from me." But He knows those who are in His fold and each one of us, as His sheep, are of great value to Him. This is seen in the parable found in Luke 15 where Jesus tells of a shepherd who was responsible for the care of 100 sheep. One of his sheep strayed away from the fold. When the shepherd discovered this, he immediately left the 99 sheep safe in the fold and went searching for the one lost sheep until he found it. This parable is a powerful illustration of how nothing escapes His attention in our lives as members of His flock. He knows our needs, our weaknesses, and our problems including our mistakes, such as wandering off from the flock. But He not only knows His sheep, but He also loves his sheep.

Second, The Good Shepherd Loves His Sheep.

How do we know this? Consider the words of Jesus in the tenth chapter of John's Gospel:

"I am the good shepherd. The good shepherd lays down his life for the sheep". (John 10:11)

"Just as the Father knows me and I know the Father; and I lay down my life for the sheep." (John 10:15)

"For this reason, the Father loves me, because I lay down my life that I may take it up again." (John 10:17)

"No one takes it from me, but I lay it down of my own accord. I have authority to lay it down, and I have authority to take it up again." (John 10:18)

In Israel, the shepherd was totally responsible for the care and welfare of his sheep. An honorable shepherd was pledged to guard and protect his sheep even at the risk of his own life. It was not an uncommon event for a shepherd to lay down his life to protect his sheep. This is the greatest expression of love when a person willingly dies to save others. This is what the Good Shepherd of the universe said in John 15:13, "Greater love has no one than this, that someone lay down his life for his friends. You are my friends..." And wonder of wonders, this is what the sinless Son of God did for rebellious sinners like you and me. We were like the one lost sheep that Jesus spoke of in His parable from Luke 15. This says to me that if you or I had been the only person lost that our heavenly shepherd would have come to earth to rescue you and/or me.

Look at Romans 5:6-8, "For while we were still weak, at the right time Christ died for the ungodly. For one will scarcely die for a righteous person—though perhaps for a good person one would dare even to die —but God shows his love for us in that while we were still sinners, Christ died for us."

We must never forget that our Good Shepherd's death was voluntary. He was not some poor victim caught up in circumstances beyond His control. He foreknew what would happen to Him and yet he knowingly and willingly laid down his life for us.

David Jeremiah, in his book, "The Jesus You May Not Know", relates the following story that illustrates this kind of love. At the end of the Second World War, as the troops were returning to America, a mother went down to the port to meet her son who was coming home from battle. She wasn't prepared for the extent of his injuries, and as the boys came down the gangplanks and were brought down in wheelchairs, she looked everywhere for her son. Finally, she saw him. She could hardly grasp the extent of his injuries. He could not see her, because he had lost his eyesight. He could not stand up to greet her because he had lost his legs, nor could he put his arms around her because they were also gone.

The devastated woman began to sob and cried in deep anguish, "This terrible and cruel war! You've lost your eyes, and you've lost your legs, and you've lost your arms!" Her son raised himself as best he could and said to his grieving mother, " Oh, no, Mother, don't say that. Lost them? No, no, no! Mother, I *gave* them on behalf of my country!

Likewise, Jesus did not lose his life! He gave it away on behalf of all of us. He voluntarily laid down His life so that He could conquer the power of death, and through His victory He could give to all of His followers eternal life, including a new glorified resurrected body!

Ponder this for a moment, my friend. You are loved! You are loved by the Great I Am, the Shepherd of the Universe. And the proof of this is seen on a hill called Calvary. When Jesus the Good Shepherd became as a lamb that was slaughtered for our sins, He was not some poor victim caught up in circumstances beyond His understanding. He was not forced or driven to Calvary against His will. He did it willingly. He said that no one took His life but rather He chose to lay it down. He was compelled by His great love for his sheep. So, the Good Shepherd knows and loves His sheep, and this includes you and me.

Third, The Good Shepherd Provides for His sheep.

Look again at the description of the Good Shepherd in verse 9, Jesus said "…If anyone enters by me, he will be saved and will go in and out and find pasture." Remember the words of Psalm 23:1-3, " The Lord is my shepherd; I shall not want. He makes me lie down in green pastures. He leads me beside the still waters. He restores my soul. He leads me in the paths of righteousness for His name's sake."

One of the primary jobs of a shepherd was to make certain that the sheep received proper nourishment and rest. I am sure that many who are reading these words remember being required either in college or high school to read Abraham Maslow's "hierarchy of needs".

Maslow suggested that we humans have five basic needs:

1) Physiological Needs - This refers to the basic requirements needed to maintain physical life (food, water, etc.).

2) Safety Needs - People need to feel safe and secure.

3) Social Needs - People need to love and be loved. We need to feel accepted and have a sense of belonging.

4) Esteem Needs - People need to have a sense of worth and significance. We need to believe that our lives have value and meaning.

5) Self-Actualization Needs - People need to develop, learn and mature physically, mentally, emotionally and socially. We all have an innate need to achieve, and to have a sense of accomplishment; to be all we can be. I mentioned that he called this list a "hierarchy of needs". So, first, we have physical needs to be met for survival. After these needs are met, the next step in the hierarchy is safety, etc.

I believe our Good Shepherd cares about all these basic human needs and through His grace He will supply all our needs according to His will and plan for each of our lives. This does not mean that we will never suffer and struggle at times in this fallen world. Jesus was perfect, and yet consider all the suffering He endured while He walked upon this planet. But what it does mean is that because He took on Himself all the evil and hatred in this fallen world, and even died due to a horrible crucifixion, He arose from the dead as the victor. And as we look to Him in faith as our Lord and Savior, He will provide the grace and help we need to get through whatever the devil and the fallen world throws at us.

But this does not relieve us of our own personal responsibility to meet our own needs and the needs of others. The Apostle James wrote in his book in the New Testament that "faith without works is dead" in James

2:17. But nevertheless this faith is not ultimately a faith in ourselves, but it is faith in the Good Shepherd, who out of His infinite wisdom will provide the resources and arrange the circumstances for our needs to be met. We are promised in Philippians 4:19, "And my God will supply every need of yours according to his riches in glory in Christ Jesus." Changing metaphors from shepherds to parents, note what Jesus said in His famous Sermon on the Mount, in Matthew 7:11, "If you then, who are evil (sinful), know how to give good gifts to your children, how much more will your Father who is in heaven give good things to those who ask Him."

Now I am sure that some who read the list by Maslow immediately noticed a glaring omission. He made no reference to spiritual needs. This is because he was a secular Jew who was a brilliant man, but to my knowledge he did not address the spiritual condition of humanity. But I think we can still benefit from his insight into how we humans function physically, emotionally and psychologically. However, the greatest need for every human being is to make a personal commitment to Jesus, the Good Shepherd, and the result will be a blessed assurance of having received the gift of eternal life.

Fourth, The Good Shepherd Protects His Sheep.

Notice the incredible words of Jesus that assure His sheep of eternal security in John 10:12-14, "He who is a hired hand and not a shepherd, who does not own the sheep, sees the wolf coming and leaves the sheep and flees, and the wolf snatches them and scatters them. He flees because he is a hired hand and cares nothing for the sheep. I am the good shepherd. I know my own and they know me, just as the Father knows me and I know the Father; and I lay down my life for the sheep". Later on in the same chapter we see the nature of His commitment to secure the destiny of His sheep: John 10:27-30, "My sheep hear my voice, and I know them, and they follow me. I give them eternal life, and they will never perish, and no one will snatch them out of my hand. My Father, who has given them to me, is greater than all, and no one is able to snatch them out of my Father's hand. I and the Father are one."

What an overwhelming mind-blowing statement by Jesus!! Don't forget that when Jesus spoke these wonderful words, He had before Him the horrific suffering and death by crucifixion on a Roman cross. Yet He had absolute trust in the Father that beyond the anguish of the cross awaited a glorious resurrection after which He would ascend back to the Father in heaven. Look at what Jesus prayed not long before he was crucified, in John 17:5, 10-11a, "And now, Father, glorify me in your own presence with the glory that I had before the world existed...All mine are yours and yours are mine, and I am glorified in them. And I am no longer in the world, but they are in the world, and I am coming to you. Holy Father, keep them in your name, which you have given me..." This is a powerful section of what has been traditionally called "The High Priestly Prayer", in which prior to Christ's arrest and crucifixion, He prayed for His current followers, plus all His future followers in the ages that followed. He prayed for our eternal security. He prayed that we would be one as He and the Father are one. What a glorious prayer!

But the picture in John 10 is that just as a faithful human shepherd was committed to protecting his sheep how much more so is this true of our Divine Shepherd in heaven. Let us reflect on the incredible description in Psalm 23:4, "Even though I walk through the valley of the shadow of death, I will fear no evil, for you are with me; your rod and your staff, they comfort me." Those who have been to Israel can picture in their minds the Judean desert which have these winding roads through valleys which made both humans and sheep very vulnerable to attack.

As a youngster, David, the writer of this psalm, tended his father's sheep and was very familiar with the dangers potentially lurking within these valleys. It reminded him of the dangers we face as believers, but he had a confidence that just as the Lord enabled him to use his rod and staff to protect his sheep, he also was convinced that the Lord would protect him spiritually as well as he walked through the spiritually dark places in this world. The "rod" he mentions was a short stick which was heavy on one end and often had nails driven into the heavy end. It was used as kind of a club to defend the sheep when a wild animal attacked the flock. The "staff" was a long stick with a crook on one end. It served as a good walking stick, but its primary purpose was to be used to rescue sheep when one was caught in a thicket or a crevice. As the sheep followed their shepherd through deep dark valleys where danger was always potentially lurking, the shepherd was alert and ever ready to protect and rescue his sheep.

And so it is with our Good Shepherd, the Lord Jesus. He doesn't always prevent us from facing dangerous situations, but when they do come, which is inevitable, He will not forsake us like the hireling. Now this especially applies to our spiritual protection. No matter what comes against us, we are spiritually safe and eternally secure in the care of the Good Shepherd. Remember the words we read earlier in John 10:27-28, where Jesus said, "My sheep hear my voice, and I know them, and they follow me. I give them eternal life and they will never perish, and no one can snatch them out my hand."

But this protection also applies to us physically if it fulfills His plans for our service while still on earth. Unless Jesus returns during our lifetime to rapture us, we all will die. We are not immune from the effects of living in a fallen world, but even in those times of stress and pain, the Good Shepherd comes to us. As the 23rd Psalm says, "Even though I walk through the valley of the shadow of death, I will fear no evil, for you are with; your rod and staff, they comfort me." We can trust Him to lead us down the right path. It is a path of provision, and protection, and ultimately a path to eternal perfection. He is leading us on a journey to maturity, completeness and holiness; it is a path to Glory! Yes, there is a glorious eternal destiny awaiting all sheep in His flock. Even in suffering He will protect our souls. No matter what happens we are safe in His care even at physical death. I love the words of Paul in Philippians 1:6 where he wrote, "And I am sure of this, that he who began a good work in you will bring it to completion at the day of Jesus Christ."

Fifth, The Good Shepherd Leads His Sheep.

Let's look again at John 10:3-5, "...The sheep hear his voice, and he calls his own sheep by name and leads them out. When he has brought out all his own, he goes before them, and the sheep follow him, for they know his voice. A stranger they will not follow, but they flee from him, for they do not know the voice of strangers." But note another aspect of what Jesus later says in John 10:27, "My sheep hear my voice, and I know them, and they follow me." You see, a shepherd in Israel never drove his sheep like cattle, but rather he was out in the front leading them and the sheep knew him and followed him. Remember that the Good Shepherd in Psalm 23:3 says of himself that he leads me in the paths of righteousness for His name's sake. This literally is best translated, "He leads me in the right paths...". So, we can trust Him to lead us down the right path. He will lead us to a path of provision, and of protection, and ultimately a path to perfection in glory. He is leading us on a journey to maturity, completeness and holiness. It is indeed a path to glory. There is a glorious destiny awaiting all the sheep of his flock.

But as He leads us down this right path, we must always keep in perspective that the ultimate glory goes to Him, not us. Notice the last four words of this verse which says, "for his name's sake". This statement reminds me of Isaiah 43:7 which says, "Everyone who is called by my name whom I created for my glory; I formed him, yes, I have made him."

Now in the light of this marvelous truth that the Good Shepherd leads his sheep down a path to glory, let's lastly consider:

3. THE GOOD SHEPHERD'S CALL

First, Let's focus on The Reach of His Call

To whom does the Good Shepherd Call? How far is the reach of His voice?

A) HE SPEAKS TO ALL THOSE WITHIN HIS FOLD.

> Look again at John 10:3, "To him (The Good Shepherd) the gatekeeper opens. The sheep hears his voice, and he calls his own sheep by name and leads them out". So, the Shepherd communicates with His sheep. He also has much to say to us modern sheep today, if we are focused and listening.

> Let's look once again at John 10:27, "My sheep hear my voice, and I know them, and they follow me."

> How can He lead us if He is not speaking? Some people have the mistaken idea that God only spoke in Biblical times, and once the Bible was completed, He never spoke again. Well, this is true in the sense of new doctrinal revelation being given, as if the Bible was incomplete and periodically needed updated. This is clearly a lie. It says in 2 Timothy 3:16 says, "All scripture is breathed out by God and profitable for teaching, for reproof, for correction, and for training in righteousness." So, the Bible is sufficient and needs no new revelation to supplement what God has already revealed and recorded as the basic doctrines for the Christian faith. But God is still speaking today through the truth of scripture and the Holy Spirit who indwells every believer in Jesus.

> The way the Spirit speaks today is through an inner prompting or a conviction deep within our souls. He takes the truth already revealed in the scripture and applies it in a personal way to the lives of His sheep. Scripture is filled with instruction, principles and laws which reveal the truth by which we are to order our lives.

Psalm 119:11 says," I have stored up your word in my heart, that I might not sin against you." Psalm 119:105 says, "Your word is a lamp to my feet and a light to my path." Let us not forget that the same Holy Spirit who inspired the writing of the Bible, is also able to illuminate the minds and hearts of those who are open to receiving truth.

An example is the assurance of our salvation. Satan tries to sow doubts in the hearts of believers regarding the assurance that we are forever secure as children of God. But look at what the Spirit inspired Paul to write in Romans 8:14-16, "for all who are led by the Spirit of God are sons (children) of God. For you did not receive the spirit of slavery to fall back into fear, but you have received the Spirit of adoption as sons, by whom we cry, 'Abba! Father!' The Spirit himself bears witness with our spirit that we are children of God." So Paul is saying that those who struggle with the assurance of salvation can find assurance through the written Word. Typically, as we read and study the scriptures, the Holy Spirit will take what we are reading and in His still small voice will take the truth of the passage and apply it in a very personal way bringing assurance to our hearts. The Spirit will also speak through people, prayer and circumstances. But it will always be consistent with the written Word of God. Our Lord never contradicts Himself.

I recall years ago a woman wrote some inspirational books that became Christian best sellers. Later on she left her husband for another man claiming that she had prayed about it, and that God told her it was okay. Well, she may have heard an inner prompting, but it was not the Spirit of God, because God does not contradict Himself. The seventh commandment says, "You shall not commit adultery". If this woman was genuinely saved, she obviously hardened her heart against the Spirit of God, and The Good Shepherd will come after her with some strong discipline.

B) HE ALSO SPEAKS TO THOSE OUTSIDE OF HIS FOLD.

Look at John 10:16, "And I have other sheep that are not of this fold. I must bring them also, and they will listen to my voice. So, there will be one flock, one shepherd." The Good Shepherd anticipates the continual growth of His flock. Through His foreknowledge He seeks and calls those He knows will respond to His call. He continues to seek the lost, those who wander about aimlessly, in terrible danger without the Good Shepherd. But do not miss the point I just made, notice that they don't find him, but rather He first seeks them.

To be found by the Good Shepherd, one must believe when He calls. Jesus said in John 10:26-27, "but you do not believe because you are not among my sheep. My sheep hear my voice, and I know them, and they follow me."

And so, it is unbelief that keeps lost sheep out of the fold. Is He calling you? Will you choose to believe?

Second, Let's conclude by looking at The Response to His Call

We have seen the acceptable response, but how do we, who enter His flock, express that faith?

A. HIS SHEEP LISTEN FOR HIS VOICE

Jesus mentions three times in John 10 that the sheep hear His voice (verses 3, 16 and 27). The point is that to respond to His call, we must be listening. There must be an openness to His voice and a genuine desire to hear and obey His instructions. We must seek to tune out the noise and the distractions of the world as well as its voices clamoring for our attention. This takes real discipline and commitment. This is true of human communication. It is a lot easier to talk than to listen. This is why it is important to have quiet times before the Lord on a regular basis, and during these times meditate upon the scriptures with an openness to the Spirit of God in His "still small voice" teaching and guiding you.

Another important discipline is to intentionally practice the presence of God throughout the day. Paul wrote that we should pray without ceasing. He was obviously not suggesting that we should be on our knees continuously praying every moment we are awake, but what I do believe he was instructing his readers to do was to consciously be open to God's presence every day. I communicate with God all throughout each day. I thank Him; I worship Him; I periodically ask for wisdom, for strength, for forgiveness, and I pray for the needs of others as people come to mind. And I also listen for the prompting of my spirit by His Spirit. Jesus would occasionally say, "He who has ears to hear, let him hear!" He said this when He was on earth teaching with an audible voice, but this still applies today as He speaks through the truth of the scriptures by means of the inner voice of the Holy Spirit who indwells every born-again believer.

This clearly implies that:

B. HIS SHEEP KNOW HIS VOICE

Let us remind ourselves again of what Jesus said in John 10:3b-5, "...The sheep hear his voice, and he calls his own sheep by name and leads them out. When he has brought out all his own, he goes before them, and the sheep follow him, for they know his voice. A stranger they will not follow, but they will flee from him, for they do not recognize the voice of strangers."

This is such a powerful analogy. The sheep immediately recognize the voice of their shepherd. And this is also true at another level in our relationship with Jesus, our Good Shepherd. His sheep are able to distinguish His voice from the voice of strangers. These strangers include Satan and his demons as well as the ungodly influences of a fallen world. The devil even tries to mimic the voice

85

of the Good Shepherd. The key to not getting deceived by the evil one, is to know the Good Shepherd so well that you can always recognize whether the words, ideas and impressions coming into your mind are truly from the Good Shepherd or some other source. So, this clearly implies that we need to get to know our Good Shepherd as well as possible.

Well, how does this happen? Especially with regard to an infinite being like God? Obviously, it requires faith, plus a knowledge of God's written word. A study of God's Word reveals the attributes, the character, the ways, and the great purposes of the Divine Shepherd. I believe the more we learn about God as a person the more we will recognize when His Spirit is guiding or prompting us. We have all heard stories of people doing horrific things and later they said God told them to do it. Well, they may have thought that God was speaking to them, but notice that Jesus said, I am "the", not "a", Good Shepherd. He is the one and only true Good Shepherd. And so, once again, we are confronted, as is true of all His 'I AM" statements, with an astounding claim. Jesus of Nazareth clearly claimed to be the one and only Shepherd of Israel who is the Lord God of the universe. And so, the bottom line is this—He is who He claimed to be, or He was insanely deceived, or a deceiver. The "I AM sayings" of Jesus leave no middle ground.

How do we get to know a person? By spending time with that person. This is true of our relationship with Jesus. As we spend time in prayer and worship; the study of God's Word; and meaningful fellowship with others who know the Good Shepherd; we also begin to learn more about His ways, His character, His attributes and His great purposes.

When I was a young person still living at home, there was a friend of our family who would occasionally call to speak with my dad. If I answered the phone, He would sometimes disguise his voice by mimicking other people we both knew. But I quickly figured out that this was not the person he claimed to be. He was very good at disguising his voice, but if he made statements or used phrases that were not consistent with the person he was mimicking, I quickly said, "Bill, I know it is you". Likewise, the greater our knowledge of Jesus, the better we will become in recognizing His voice as He speaks to our souls.

I have had counseling sessions with people over the years who struggled with discerning whether an inner prompting is from the Lord or not. Let's review in summary some principles I have already touched on. First, God will typically speak to us through His written Word, as we read, meditate and listen to the preaching of God's Word. His Spirit will convict us of a sin we need to confess, or challenge us with a new truth we need to remember, or call us to obey an assignment He has put on our hearts, or correct us on a misunderstanding or wrong interpretation of Biblical doctrine. Search the Scriptures to make sure that the idea or prompting you have sensed is consistent with God's written word.

If you are a new believer, find a spiritually mature believer, and ask this person if they would be willing to mentor you, or find a Bible teaching church that has a mentoring program for new believers.

Several years ago, I came across the following story. During World War I, some Turkish soldiers tried to steal a flock of sheep from a hillside near Jerusalem. The shepherd, who had been sleeping, suddenly awakened to see his sheep being driven off on the other side of the ravine. He could not hope to recapture his flock by force single-handedly, but suddenly he had an idea. Standing on his side of the ravine, he put his hands to his mouth and gave his own peculiar call, which he used each day to gather his sheep, to him. The sheep heard the familiar sound. For a moment they listened and then, hearing it again, they turned and rushed down one side of the ravine and up the other toward their shepherd. It was impossible for the soldiers to stop the animals. The shepherd led them away to a place of safety before the soldiers could make up their minds to pursue them and all because his sheep knew their master's voice. This story illustrates a third step in a sheep's response to the Shepherd's call.

C. HIS SHEEP FOLLOW HIS VOICE

Remember, the claim by Jesus that He is THE GOOD SHEPHERD, is a claim to be the Great I Am, Yahweh, the Lord God who rules the universe. He has the position and authority to call upon whomever He pleases to come and follow Him. And we have seen in the study of the Scriptures that when we follow Him, He will lead us down the paths of righteousness which will one day enable us to dwell in the house of the Lord forever. True faith is expressed in our attitudes and actions. Notice that Jesus said His sheep will follow Him. This is the evidence or proof that they are His. The flock of God are on a journey, following Him, as our Good Shepherd. This is how Christian conversion begins. We hear deep in our soul the call of the Good Shepherd, and we decide to trust in Him as our Lord and Savior. The evidence of our genuine decision is obedience, and how we totally trust and follow Him day by day.

Five

"I Am the Resurrection and the Life"

John 11:21-27, "'Martha said to Jesus, ' Lord, if you had been here, my brother would not have died. But even now I know that whatever you ask from God, God will give you.' Jesus said to her, 'Your brother will rise again.' Martha said to him, 'I know he will rise again in the resurrection on the last day.' Jesus said to her, 'I am the resurrection and the life. Whoever believes in me, though he may die, yet shall he live, and everyone who lives and believes in me shall never die. Do you believe this?'" She said to him, 'Yes, Lord; I believe that you are the Christ, the Son of God, who is coming into the world.'"

John 11:33-44 - "When Jesus saw her weeping, and the Jews who had come with her also weeping, he was deeply moved in his spirit and greatly troubled. And he said, "Where have you laid him?" They said to him, "Lord, come and see." Jesus wept. So the Jews said, "See how he loved him!" But some of them said, "Could not he who opened the eyes of the blind man also have kept this man from dying?" Then Jesus, deeply moved again, came to the tomb. It was a cave, and a stone lay against it.

Jesus said, "Take away the stone." Martha, the sister of the dead man, said to him, "Lord, by this time there will be an odor, for he has been dead four days." Jesus said to her, "Did I not tell you that if you believed you would see the glory of God?" So they took away the stone. And Jesus lifted up his eyes and said, "Father, I thank you that you have heard me. I knew that you always hear me, but I said this on account of the people standing around, that they may believe that you sent me." When he had said these things, he cried out with a loud voice, "Lazarus, come out." The man who had died came out, his hands and feet bound with linen strips, and his face wrapped with a cloth. Jesus said to them, "Unbind him, and let him go."

One evening the great conductor, Arturo Toscanini, conducted Beethoven's Ninth Symphony. It was a masterful performance! At the conclusion, the audience went wild in expressing their appreciation and adoration of the great musician. As Toscanini stood there, he bowed and bowed, and then he acknowledged his orchestra. When the ovation finally began to subside, he turned and looked at his musicians, and with great intensity and yet in a whisper, he said, "Gentlemen! Gentlemen!" The orchestra leaned forward to listen. Toscanini said, "Gentlemen, I am nothing!" This was an extraordinary admission since Toscanini was known to have an enormous ego. Then he added, "Gentlemen, you are nothing!" But then with great adoration, he said, "But Beethoven is everything, everything, everything!" He knew that without Beethoven's music they could not have reached such heights musically. And this is what I have been attempting to communicate in this book about Jesus, the great I AM, who came to connect with us fallen creatures.

Jesus Christ is everything! This is why I titled this book 'The Unique Supremacy of Jesus'. Because of who He is, only He is able and sufficient to meet the needs of the human soul. The "I am" sayings of Jesus clearly tell us this. He claims to be "the", not "a", Good

Shepherd. He is the one and only true Good Shepherd. And so, once again, we are confronted with an astounding claim about Jesus of Nazareth. He clearly claimed to be the one and only Shepherd of Israel who is the Lord God of the universe. He is who He claimed to be, or was either deceived or a deceiver. The "I AM sayings" of Jesus leave no middle ground. 'The Bread of Life', 'The Light of the World', and 'The Good Shepherd' (of our souls) are three examples of the audacious claims Jesus made about Himself. But He not only made such claims, but He backed them up with His amazing words and actions. This is why I have titled this book, 'The Unique Supremacy of Jesus.' The Apostle Paul summed it up in Philippians 1:21a, where he wrote, 'For to me to live is Christ'.

But if you are a follower of Jesus, have there been moments in your life when you prayed, 'Lord, where were you, when I needed you?" You found yourself in a desperate situation, and you called out to Him for help and from your perspective He did not come through. In that moment, He did not seem to be, nor feel like your everything. Well, here in John 11, we find similar sentiments expressed by two of Jesus' closest friends, Martha, and her sister Mary. Their brother, Lazarus, had become terribly ill. This family was remarkably close to Jesus. He typically stayed with them when He visited Jerusalem. This was because they lived in the village of Bethany which was about 2 miles southeast of the Holy City on the eastern slope of the Mount of Olives.

In verses 1-2 we are introduced to the family and the problem that confronted them. Their brother, Lazarus, had become very ill and their immediate response is summed up in verse 3, "So the sisters sent to him, saying, 'Lord, he whom you love is ill.'" Notice they did not make a specific request for Jesus to come. They simply informed Jesus of their brother's serious condition, and were confident that once He knew, He would come quickly. Notice also that Jesus and Lazarus were very close friends, because the sisters did not identify the name of Lazarus, but simply said, "He whom you love is ill."

The response of Jesus was initially very confusing to his disciples. He first said, "This illness does not lead to death. It is for the glory of God, so that the Son of God may be glorified through it." But then in verse 5, John emphasizes how much Jesus loved the two sisters as well as Lazarus. However, in verse 6, John tells us that after Jesus heard the report of the seriousness of His friend's condition, He did a startling thing. He remained two more days before He left to go to Judea, where the home of Lazarus was located. The disciples were quite reluctant to return because many of the Jewish leaders had tried to stone Him the last time He was there. But notice what Jesus said in response to their concern, "our friend Lazarus has fallen asleep, but I go to awaken him"(verse 11b).

Beginning in verse 17 through verse 44, we find recorded possibly the greatest miracle Jesus performed during His earthly ministry. John tells us that when Jesus arrived, He was told that Lazarus had been in the tomb four days. Someone informed the two sisters that Jesus was on His way, so when Martha learned that Jesus was near, she went out and met Him. But Mary remained in their house. The first thing Martha said to Him upon His arrival was, " Lord, if you would have been here, my brother would not have died" (verse 21). These were strong words from Martha. But then she softened the impact a little by following up with an affirmation of hope. Note what she said next, but even now I know that whatever you ask from God, God will give you."

Nevertheless, she was obviously confused by what she perceived to be negligence on the part of Jesus. Her question implied a degree of doubt. She was asking, Lord, where have you been? If you had come immediately after I sent word to you, none of this would have happened. Why didn't you respond immediately, when we so desperately needed you? Most believers have had moments in their lives when they have had similar confusion. I know that I have.

The story found here in John 11 reveals some truths that ought to encourage us when we are confronted with similar doubts or questions. So, join me as we look at what Jesus said in this passage which can help us deal with doubt and confusion. The first truth to remember is this:

1. CHRIST DOES CARE.

In times of deep sorrow and intense disappointment we are prone to question and ask if He really cares.

But a study of the New Testament makes it clear that indeed He does care even when our immediate circumstances may provoke in us feelings of doubt and abandonment. But as we look at the bigger picture, we find in God's Word multiple examples and assurances that indeed He does care deeply about our welfare and looks upon us with compassion.

Note what the two sisters said when they sent word to Jesus about their brother's illness; the message was simple but straightforward, and it said, "Lord, he whom you love is ill" (John 11: 3). The Greek word that John used to translate the sister's reference to the love that Jesus had for Lazarus was the verb "philia" which speaks of emotional affection. But note how John in verse 5, employed another Greek word used by Jesus in reference to Lazarus which expressed a selfless sacrificial love for Lazarus. The verb is "agape" which involves much more than emotional affection. It is an unconditional commitment to pursue the highest good of another person no matter what the cost.

As John writes after the fact, he knew with an absolute certainty that Jesus loved Lazarus, and so His decision to not immediately go to Bethany and wait two more days was rooted in love. Now, in the heightened emotion of the moment, the response of Jesus appeared to be insensitive. But in hindsight, He was not at all, when a person steps back and looks at the whole picture. There was a good reason Jesus waited, as we shall see later.

And so, even when it appears the Lord has let you down, do not jump to conclusions prematurely. Keep in perspective that the Lord never makes mistakes. His love for us is a devotion ruled by infinite wisdom. There is always a reason. We must learn to trust that in His love, He will always do what is best.

But let me hasten to add that this does not mean that our great God is devoid of emotion. His love is not cold calculation, nor reason without feeling. Even though Jesus, as God incarnate, knew what He was doing and delayed responding to his friends needs for a reason, even though Jesus would literally raise Lazarus from the dead, He was deeply moved when He did arrive.

In verses 32-35, John tells us that "when Mary came to where Jesus was and saw him, she fell at his feet, saying to him, 'Lord if you had been here, my brother would not have died. When Jesus saw her weeping, he was deeply moved in his spirit and greatly troubled. And he said, 'Where have you laid him?' They said to him, "Lord, come and see.' Jesus wept." Later, verse 38 says, 'Then Jesus, deeply moved again, came to the tomb. It was a cave, and a stone lay against it.'"

Different interpretations have been given as to why Jesus responded with such intense emotion. I believe that Jesus was experiencing two basic emotions. First, He experienced grief. He was identifying with His friends as they felt such deep sorrow and a sense of loss. He grieved with them as they dealt with the harsh reality of death. But, along with grief, He also expressed anger. Note again in verse 38, John writes that "Jesus, deeply moved, came to the tomb." Many Greek scholars believe the phrase 'deeply moved', is better translated 'was indignant'. It does not convey the idea of uncontrolled anger, but more of a deep sense of righteous anger or rage that compels a person to correct a wrong or an injustice. So, yes, Christ does care! This leads to a second truth to keep in perspective.

2. CHRIST IS IN CONTROL.

We not only wrestle with the question, 'does he care?', but when we face overwhelming difficulties such as sickness and sorrow we are tempted to question if He really is in charge, and able to meet our needs. Many people who profess to be Christ followers have had painful events occur in their lives and they often have asked, "If the Lord is in control, then why did He let this horrible thing happen in my life?" Mary and Martha, no doubt wondered, why did Jesus allow Lazarus to die?

Well, there are not simple pat answers as to why our Lord sometimes ordains (or allows) painful things to happen in our lives and other times He intervenes and works a miracle. But this much we can know with certainty; our Sovereign Lord is in control. He always has been, and He always will be. Nothing ever catches Him by surprise! Now, many have asked, "Does this mean that He causes everything that happens? Well, for centuries sincere believers have debated this question. But we know He lives in the eternal present and sees the future as clearly as he does the past.

There is nothing in our text which indicates that God directly caused Lazarus to get sick and die; however, Christ is the second Person of the divine Trinity (Father, Son and Holy Spirit). This means that all three persons of the Godhead have the same divine attributes. This also means that like the Father, and like the Spirit, Christ is also sovereign. He is the incarnation of the Great I Am. In Matthew 28:18a Jesus said, "All authority in heaven and on earth has been given to me." He is the Lord over all circumstances. And nothing ever happens outside His permissive will. Everything that happens, regardless of the cause, has been foreknown and foreordained by the triune God to be used for His great purpose.

Note what Jesus said to his disciples after Mary and Martha sent word to him about Lazarus' critical illness; "This illness does not lead to death. It is for the glory of God, so that the Son of God may be glorified through it." Jesus did not mean that Lazarus would not die. In fact, Lazarus died at about the same time the message of Lazarus' illness arrived. Keep in mind that the distance between Bethany and where Jesus was located was about a day's journey. After Jesus received the message, He remained where He was for two more days, and in verse 4 He made it clear is that death does not have the final word. Jesus was fully aware of what was happening, and so He finally took the day's journey to Bethany. This amounts to a total of four days. Notice in verse 17 we are told that Lazarus had been dead four days when Jesus arrived. What Jesus meant by His earlier statement was that He had the situation under control. There was a reason for the sickness and death of Lazarus, as well as for delay of Jesus. God the Father wanted Jesus to use this as an opportunity to display His Son's great glory. Remember what Jesus said earlier in verse 4 after the sisters sent word to Him about their brother's illness. He said, "This illness does not lead to death. It is for the glory of God, so that the Son of God may be glorified through it." And so, Jesus did not get anxious, nor did He panic. Let us keep in perspective who Jesus was and is. He is God the Son, the second person of the Godhead. He intended to use what appeared to be a tragic situation for the greater good.

A further indication that Christ was in control can be observed in verses 7-10. In verse 7, Jesus said to His disciples, "let us go to Judea again". In verse 8, the disciples said to him, "Rabbi, the Jews were just now seeking to stone you, and you are going there again?" In verses 9-10, Jesus answered, "Are there not 12 hours in the day? If anyone walks in the day, he does not stumble, because he sees the light of this world. But if anyone walks in the night, he stumbles, because the light is not in him." And so, the disciples were saying, "Rabbi, Judea is hostile! They want to kill you in that region".

But Jesus was not shaken by these concerns expressed by His followers, but He responded with calm dignity and confidence. He simply said, "Our friend Lazarus has fallen asleep, but I go to awaken him". Well, once again the disciples were totally confused, and their response was, "Lord, if he has fallen asleep, he will recover." In verse 13, John explains that Jesus was speaking of Lazarus' death, but they thought He meant Lazarus was taking rest in sleep. So in verses 14-15, John wrote the following words; "Then Jesus told them plainly, 'Lazarus has died, and for your sake I am glad that I was not there, so that you may believe. But let us go to him.' So Thomas, called the twin, said to his fellow disciples. "Let us also go, that we may die with him." Ah, Thomas was always the pessimist, but in this moment, he felt a great courage and was ready to go and die with Jesus.

Now we must remember that none of this caught Jesus by surprise. He was orchestrating it all, knowing that He must go to the cross to die in our place for our sins. He was in control of the entire situation. But notice again what He said immediately after verse 15, "and for your sake I am glad that I was not there, so that you may believe. But let us go to him." Wow!

3. CHRIST ALWAYS COMES.

In this passage we just read, we find a clue as to why Jesus does not always intervene at the time we have requested. He has a better plan and for this plan to unfold the timing is critical. Christ always comes when we need Him. But when He comes, it is always at the exact right moment according to His infinite wisdom. This is why He could say, "I am glad that I was not there". By allowing Lazarus to die and not coming to visit his sisters until four days after his death, the timing was right for Jesus to do two things:

First, He comes at that moment when He will receive the greatest glory!

Now here is a key to understanding the purpose of everything that Almighty God has created. This is the nature of reality. This is not because God is on some gigantic ego trip. To paraphrase Bruce Ware, "Life is not about us, but it is all about God". 1 Corinthians 10:31 says, "So, whether you eat or drink, or whatever you do, do it all to the glory of God"; Romans 11:36 says, "For from him, and through him, to him are all things. To him be the glory forever!"; Isaiah 43:7 says, "Everyone who is called by my name whom I have created for my glory; I formed him, yes, I have made him." Jesus said in the Sermon on the Mount, "Let your light so shine before men, that they may see your good works and glorify your Father in heaven."

Forgive me for using an illustration from sports, but hopefully this will help us understand the concept of glory in human terms. Most people, including those who do not typically follow sports, are familiar with the name Tom Brady. Why? Because of his amazing exploits as a quarterback in the NFL. Football fans know that Tom Brady was especially famous because of his ability to bring his team back during the last two minutes of a football game to win. Just when it appeared that his team would lose, he would lead them down the field to a victory during a game ending drive by throwing a touchdown. Now during these moments, the crowd would erupt with applause and shouts of praise for Tom Brady. Within reason I see nothing wrong with people getting excited and cheering for their sports heroes. In these dramatic moments the focus was on Tom and his ability.

The point is that if we can get this excited over sports heroes, how much more so should we be praising and rejoicing over the greatness of our triune God. It is not that the Lord is on an ego trip, nor does He need our praise to feel good about Himself. But everything in God's creation exists for His glory. This is simply the nature of reality. And so, when everything is God-centered, creation functions properly and God's creatures are fulfilled and joyful. For our own well-being, it is important that God gets the glory. We all win when He is glorified. I love John Piper's statement on this theme when he wrote, "God is most glorified in us, when we are most satisfied in Him".

Well, since the coming of Christ to this earth, the Father is most glorified through the Son. This is how prayer is answered. Look at what Jesus said John 14:13, " Whatever you ask in my name, this I will do, that the Father may be glorified in the Son." Now, look at what

Jesus said in verse 4 regarding the death of Lazarus, "This illness does not lead to death. It is for the glory of God, so that the Son of God may be glorified through it." Jesus waited so that when He did arrive Lazarus would be indisputably dead. His body was already in the process of decay. He waited until the situation seemed hopeless and then intervened.

Beginning in verse 38 through verse 44, we read the amazing drama of this incredible miracle. "Then Jesus, deeply moved again, came to the tomb. It was a cave, and a stone lay against it. Jesus said, "Take away the stone." Martha, the sister of the dead man, said to Him, "Lord, by this time there will be an odor, for he has been dead four days." Jesus said to her, " Did I not tell you that if you believed you would see the glory of God? So they took away the stone. And Jesus lifted his eyes and said, 'Father, I thank you that you have heard. I knew that you always hear me, but I said this on account of the people standing around, that they may believe that you sent me." When he said these things, he cried out with a loud voice, "Lazarus, come out" The man who had died came out, his hands and feet bound with linen strips, and his face wrapped with a cloth. Jesus said to them, "Unbind him, and let him go."

Wow!!! The only explanation was that God did this! No man other than Jesus Christ, the God-Man, should get the glory! The only response that seemed appropriate was to worship and glorify God through his Son!

Now the Lord is still setting up situations today designed to maximize our worship and praise of Him. Not typically through raising the dead, for this was a unique historical event as a sign validating the identity of Jesus. But He is still responding to the prayers of His followers through intervening in our lives in such a way that He alone gets the glory.

Second, He comes at the exact moment when He will have the greatest impact.

Christ waited and then came at just the right moment when He could have a maximum effect upon the disciples as well as the family and friends of Lazarus. Notice again what Jesus said in verses 14b-15, "...Lazarus has died, and for your sake I am glad that I was not there, so that you may believe. But let us go to him." Note again that he says, "for your sake", and then adds "that you may believe". It is clear that a primary goal of Jesus was to build the faith of His disciples.

We also see that this was His stated goal in the prayer that He prayed to the Father. Let us be reminded of what he prayed in verses 41b-42: "And Jesus lifted up His eyes and said, "Father, I thank you that you have heard me. I knew that you always hear me, but I said this on account of the people standing around, that they may believe that you sent me." Look at the results recorded in verse 45, "Many of the Jews therefore, who had come with Mary, and had seen what he did, believed in Him." The point is that God is always doing things to develop and strengthen our faith, because faith is absolutely the key to experiencing God and His power in our lives.

Several years ago, I left my home to make a hospital visit during a cold winter evening, and upon arrival I parked in the hospital's parking garage. At that time, I was driving a gray Nissan Altima. After finishing the visit, I made my way back to the garage, to the same floor and down the correct aisle. It was one of those cold wintery nights when the air just seemed to cut right through a person's body. Then I spotted the gray Nissan Altima. I rushed with great anticipation to get out of the cold and stuck my key in the door and it would not work. The key would fit in the hole, but it would not turn. I kept trying and became increasingly frustrated. As my dad used to say, I was about "to lose my religion". But the Holy Spirit helped me "to get a grip", and in that moment I looked up, and saw another gray Nissan Altima just two spaces over. I rushed over and stuck the key in the door, and it worked!

In the darkness of a cold winter night the two cars looked the same, but obviously they were not.

I share this story to illustrate a spiritual reality. The evil one is an expert counterfeiter. He will try to deceive us by imitating the blessings of God, but when one falls for his deception, we are left standing out in the cold. Always keep in mind, that there is only one key that opens the door to the warmth and safety and blessings of God's grace, and that is putting your complete trust in Jesus Christ alone as your Lord and Savior.

The key is once again faith. Hebrews 11:6 says, "And without faith it is impossible to please him, for whoever would draw near to God must believe that he exists and that he rewards those who seek him." Faith is important to God because it has to do with His character and integrity. I recall hearing Dr. Adrian Rodgers use an illustration that very effectively makes this point. He said, "Suppose I was asked to speak at a large conference and when it came time for the leader to introduce me, and he began by saying, 'Our next speaker is Dr. Adrian Rodgers, Senior pastor of Belleview Baptist Church in Memphis, Tennessee. He is an excellent preacher'.... and continues on to say some nice things about me and my ministry, but then, suppose he concludes his introduction by saying, 'but the only problem with Dr. Rodgers is that you cannot believe a word he says.'"

No matter how much praise you heap upon a person, if you question that person's integrity and trustworthiness, it undermines everything else you may have to say about him. How much more so is this true of almighty God. This is why faith is so important to Him. Now these two points, that Christ comes when He has the greatest impact, and when He gets the greatest glory, can also have the greatest positive affect upon our faith.

But why did Jesus not spare these people (Mary, Martha, friends) who loved Him, from hours of grief and disappointment? Because He waited for the moment of greatest positive impact in their lives. Out of their sorrow and desperation they learned, as never before, that you can trust the Lord no matter what happens.

4. CHRIST WILL CONQUER.

Notice in verses 21-22 the great faith that Martha still had in Jesus despite her disappointment "Martha said to Jesus, 'Lord, if you had been here, my brother would not have died. But even now I know that whatever you ask from God, God will give you." Now was Martha suggesting that Jesus raise Lazarus from dead at that very moment? Well look at what Jesus said in verse 23 in response to her great expression of faith, "Jesus said to her, 'Your brother will rise again.'" But look at her response in verse 24, "Martha said to Him, 'I know that he will rise again in the resurrection on the last day.'" Martha, as a devout Jew, was familiar with the Old Testament teaching of a resurrection of the dead at the last day. At that time the old corruptible body will be transformed into a new glorified incorruptible body. But Jesus was about to raise up Lazarus at that very moment. However, this would not be a resurrection like the last day, but rather Lazarus would be raised up with a healed body, but it would still be a physical body subject to corruption. Lazarus would die again. But in John's gospel, the miracles of Christ are called signs, which mean they signify or prophesy a future event or were object lessons designed to teach spiritual truths.

The sign behind the raising of Lazarus from the dead was stated by Jesus to Martha in verses 25-26, "Jesus said to her, "I am the resurrection and the life. Whoever believes in me, though he die, yet shall he live. And everyone who lives and believes in me shall never die. Do you believe this?" Now, let us read her marvelous profession of faith in verse 27, "She said to Him, 'Yes, Lord; I believe that you are the Christ, the Son of God, who is coming into the world.'"

When Jesus said. "I am the resurrection and the life," He was clearly stating that He was God incarnate invading this fallen world to conquer the powers of evil, sin and death! The power of God's life can overcome the deadly effects of the fallen state of humanity. And Christ's ability to raise up Lazarus from the dead signified His own more glorious resurrection that would follow his death on the cross. Through the life of God in Christ all the forces of evil against those who believe in Him can be conquered.

So, consider with me three obstacles which our Lord can conquer:

1. Christ Conquers Hopeless Circumstances

The prophet Jeremiah said, "Ah, Lord God! It is you who have made the heavens and the earth by your great power and by your outstretched arm! Nothing is too hard for you."(Jer.32:17) So, when we find ourselves in situations when all hope seems lost, don't give up. Let us be reminded again of the response of Jesus when He told those present to roll away the stone after Lazarus had been buried in a tomb four days earlier. Martha, the sister of Lazarus, protested and said 'Lord, by this time there will be an odor, for he has been dead four days." But Jesus cried out with a loud voice, 'Lazarus, come out!" He had earlier asked them to roll away the stone. Can you imagine the shock on people's faces and the sound of people gasping as they saw a man bound up like a mummy walk out of the tomb? Jesus said, "Unbind Him, and let Him go."

Look at what Jesus said to Martha after she expressed concern over Jesus asking some bystanders to take away the stone. She said, "Lord, by this time there will be an odor, for he has been dead four days." The Lord responded by saying, "Did not I tell you that if you believed you would see the glory of God?" This principle has not changed. I am not suggesting that if we believe strong enough we can see the dead raised up just as Lazarus was. But I do believe that even today we can see the glory of God revealed in circumstances which appeared to be a dead end.

If it is God's will, He can resurrect that dream to accomplish something of great significance to advance the cause of Christ that seemed dead. He can resurrect dying churches and dying marriages. And the result will be that we will see the glory of God! Yes, God can interject His resurrection power and revolutionize things to the point that the sole explanation can be that only God could have done this.

But we must trust His infinite wisdom and submit to His higher plan, and always pray "Lord, may your will be done." We must also be submissive to His perfect timing and plan. Too often when we are confronted with an overwhelming predicament, we make hasty judgements and begin to panic in what appears to be a hopeless situation, but God is still on His throne, and nothing ever catches Him by surprise. So, we must learn to trust the Lord, and expect to see the glory of God. (look again at John 11:40).

2. Christ Conquers Spiritual Death

We will look at this in more detail in the next chapter. But the bottom line is that the Bible clearly teaches that we humans in our natural state as sinners are spiritually dead in our sin. We are rebels who have a natural inclination to want to oversee our lives, as opposed to worshipping the one true God who created us for His glory. He has taken the initiative to reveal Himself to us, but in our fallen state we are separated from God, and desperately need to be reconciled to God.

This is why God the Father sent His one and only Son to the earth on a rescue mission. The gospel story is summed up in John 3:16 which says, "For God so loved the world, that he gave his only Son, that whoever believes in Him should perish but have eternal life." So, Christ is the resurrection and the life, and when we place our faith in Him, He performs a spiritual resurrection in our hearts. He literally comes to indwell us and imparts His life to us.

Baptism by immersion outwardly pictures this miraculous work of God in the souls of believers. Look at Romans 6:4-5, "We were buried therefore with Him by baptism into death, in order that, just as Christ was raised from the dead by glory of the Father, we too might walk in newness of life. For if we have been united with Him in a death like His, we shall certainly be united with Him in a resurrection like His." So, the power of resurrection is a present reality. Jesus did not say that I will be the resurrection and the life, but He said, "I am the resurrection and the life!" (John 11:25).

Right now, when a person repents of his/her sin, and invites the risen Christ into that person's heart, a miracle occurs. Through the Holy Spirit, Jesus literally comes to indwell our hearts, and imparts to us the gift of eternal life. My favorite verse in the Bible is Galatians 2:20 which says, "I have been crucified with Christ. It is no longer I who live, but Christ who lives in me. And the life I now live in the flesh I live by faith in the Son of God, who loved me, and gave himself for me."

3. Christ Conquers Physical Death

Look at John 11:25, "Jesus said to her (Martha), 'I am the resurrection and the life. Whoever believes in me, though he die, yet shall he live." Jesus in essence is saying that after He bodily returns to heaven and before He returns to this earth, we shall all experience physical death. But for a believer, death will only be a means of departing to be with Christ in heaven. Now let us look at John 11:26, "And everyone who lives and believes in me shall never die. Do you believe this?"

The Bible speaks of a second death which is eternal death and separation from God in the place called hell. The first death is physical, but those who have refused to humble themselves and open their hearts to the Lord will be consigned forever to a place of torment, darkness, and misery. But those in Christ will never truly die. We may die physically, but we continue to live. Physical death is merely the experience of our souls departing our bodies to be with Christ, awaiting the day of the resurrection of our new glorified bodies. Because Christ is "the resurrection and the life" when believers die, we go to heaven to be with Christ in a spiritual body. But then at the end of this age, "Christ will descend from heaven with a loud command, with the voice of an archangel, and with the sound of the trumpet of God. And the dead in Christ will rise first. Then we who are alive, who are left, will be caught up (raptured) together with them in the clouds to meet the Lord in the air and so we will always be the Lord." (1 Thessalonians 4:16-17) This is when we receive a new glorified body like the body of Christ Himself. In closing this chapter, I have chosen to share with you some various passages from the New Testament which the Holy Spirit inspired the Apostle Paul to write regarding our future destiny as believers in Christ.

If you are a believer, I encourage you to read these passages and let it be a time of praise and thanksgiving for the glorious destiny that our Lord has promised you.

If you have never trusted in Christ as your Lord and Savior, I encourage you to read these passages with an open heart. And if you sense that Christ is knocking on the door of your heart, speak to Him from your heart and tell Him you are sorry for your sins and invite Him to come into your life right now, as your Lord and Savior. And He will. It says in Revelation 3:20a, "Behold, I stand at the door and knock. if anyone hears my voice and opens the door, I will come in to him..."

Romans 8:18-25; I Corinthians 15:20-23; 40-44; 50-58; 2 Corinthians 5:1-8; Philippians 1:20-23; 4:20-21; 1 Thessalonians 4:13-18

Six

"I Am the Way, the Truth, and the Life"

John 14:1-9: "Let not your hearts be troubled. Believe in God; believe also in me. In my Father's house are many rooms, If it were not so, would I have told you that I go to prepare a place for you? And if I go and prepare a place for you, I will come again and will take you to myself, that where I am you may be also. And you know the way to where I am going." Thomas said to Him, "Lord, we do not know where you are going. How can we know the way?" Jesus said to him, "I am the way, and the truth, and the life. No one comes to the Father except through me, if you had known me, you would have known my Father also. From now on you know Him and have seen Him." Philip said to Him, "Lord, show us the Father, and it is enough for us." Jesus said to him, "Have I been with you so long, and you still do not know me, Philip? How can you say, 'Show us the Father"?

I f you are familiar with Toledo, Ohio and have traveled north on I 75, you no doubt have noticed a huge Islamic Mosque just south of the city. You can see the large white building just off to the right as you pass by Perrysburg, Ohio. Well, I used to pastor the First Baptist Church of Perrysburg which was located about a mile west of the mosque. We learned that at that time {the eighties) that there were 15 to 20 thousand Arabic people in the greater Toledo area. We saw this as a great mission opportunity.

So, we decided to start a mission church with the Arabic people as the focus of our outreach. "Before doing this, however, we needed to enlist a church planter who was either Arabic or could speak the Arabic language. As we began a search, the Lord miraculously opened a door for us to connect with a young man from Iraq who had just finished his studies at the Golden Gate Baptist Theological Seminary in California. His first name was Basim. He had an amazing testimony. He had been raised in a devout Muslim family. But as a young man, Basim had a longing for something more fulfilling than what Islam had given him. So, one night he said that Jesus appeared to him. This experience transformed his life. From this point on he was a committed follower of Jesus. Sadly, his family rejected him. In fact, he had to flee Iraq due to his life being threatened. He told me some harrowing stories about how he was pursued but eventually he managed to make his way to America.

After this life changing encounter with Jesus, Basim became convinced that God was calling him to be minister of the Gospel. We contacted various Southern Baptist Seminaries, and through this process we connected with him in California. He came and met with our search team, and we called him to be our mission church planter. He and his young wife moved to Perrysburg to begin their work.

From the very beginning he struggled to make connections, and he also faced some resistance in the Perrysburg community. A few months after he came, the Lord called me to go to a new field of ministry in

Dublin, Ohio. I am sure that my leaving did not help, although the church was a very loving supportive congregation. Another significant setback took place when the local clergy fellowship in Perrysburg voted to send a letter to the church requesting that they suspend their efforts to evangelize the Arabic people. They said it was offensive to the Imam and his people. The term "Imam" is used for the head or spiritual leader of a mosque. After the mosque was constructed, the Imam joined the local clergy fellowship which I had assumed was a Christian fellowship. Well, after trying for a year, Basim eventually returned to California to pastor an Arabic mission church there.

I have shared this story with you to illustrate how much our culture has changed when it comes to the perspective of people about religion. First, it illustrates how American culture has become increasingly pluralistic. In one sense, this is not a bad thing. As people, from all over the world have come to America, it seems as if God is bringing international people to our nation to give His church an opportunity to evangelize them. The hope is that when they return, or at least visit their former nation, they can share the gospel with their relatives and friends.

But as people get to know and interact with people of other religions. Those who have not been discipled through sound Biblical teaching can often get fascinated by other world religions and be led astray into false teaching. In the earlier days of our nation's history most immigrants were from Europe. But in more recent history, many immigrants came from the East, and Third World countries. This along with modern technology has exposed people to other views of reality.

This leads to a second reason for telling this story about Basim. As we become more familiar with people who sincerely practice religious beliefs different from Christianity, the question arises as to whether the Christian faith is unique among world religions. The clergy fellowship in Perrysburg concluded that sincere Muslims should be left alone. They apparently believed that either there are many ways to God or that targeting a particular group would be offensive and counterproductive. This is the question many skeptics and religious liberals ask of evangelical Christians. Many have asked, what is so special and unique about Christianity? Are there not many ways to God? If people are sincere, isn't that what matters the most?

As we consider these questions, let's first consider:

I. THE BASIC ASSERTION OF CHRISTIANITY

The assertion of Biblical Christianity is that Jesus Christ is the only way to God. This is sometimes called the exclusivity of Jesus Christ as the Savior of lost human beings. Now this belief is not something invented by the followers of Jesus. Jesus himself made this assertion in John 14:6. Shortly before He was arrested, Jesus told His disciples that He would soon leave them, but He assured them that He was returning to His Father's house and would prepare a place for them to join Him in the future. One of His disciples, Thomas, spoke up and said to Him, "Lord, we do not know where you are going. How can we know the way?" Jesus said to him, 'I am the way, and the truth, and the life. No one comes to the Father except through me.'" Notice that Jesus did not say I am a way, but "the way." In the original Greek language, the word translated "the" literally means "the one and only way" or "the exclusive way". Jesus made similar claims throughout the course of His ministry.

Look at what the Apostle Peter boldly proclaimed when he was brought before the Jewish authorities called the Sanhedrin Council. In Acts 4:12, he said, "And there is salvation in no one else, for there is no other name (Jesus) under heaven given among men by which we must be saved." This is the clear indisputable teaching of the New Testament.

Now this assertion raises some objections in the minds of many skeptics:

Objection #1) There are some who say this means that Christianity is bigoted.

By this they mean that those who believe that Jesus is the only way to God and eternal salvation, encourage its adherents to be intolerant of others who believe differently.

When a Christian makes this assertion (that Jesus is the only way), some interpret this to mean that the followers of Jesus believe that they are superior or more righteous than those who reject Jesus. Well, back in the late 90's The Southern Baptist Convention adopted a resolution which encouraged SBC churches to give more focus on evangelizing Jews. This was not a bigoted statement, but rather an expression of love for the Jewish people. Well, this made national news reports, and so shortly after the convention was over, many interpreted the resolution as bigotry toward Jews. A lot of this was stirred up not by Jewish people, but by liberals (including some Jews as well) who saw this as an opportunity to criticize the so-called narrow mindedness of evangelicals.

Well, not very long after the convention was over, I was sitting in my office trying catch up on some matters, and Karen Hopkins, our office manager, buzzed me and said there was a man on the line wanting to talk to me, and he seemed rather upset. So, I took the call, and discovered that this gentleman was very upset over the SBC resolution. He first asked me if we were an SBC church, and I said, "yes we are". And then he began to verbally attack me and our church. He said that we were bigots, and accused us of thinking we were better than Jewish people. Within my mind I prayed for the Lord to help me keep my cool and be Christlike in my response. The Holy Spirit gave me an immediate calmness. I let this man vent little bit, and then calmly, I began to address some of his accusations. I told him that we certainly do not think nor claim that we are better than the Jewish people. I told him of my travels to Israel and how the Jews have always had a special place in my heart.

I told him that I am just a sinner saved by grace, and that my Lord and Savior, Jesus, was a Jewish man, but He was also the Holy God of Israel. Well, that set him off again, and he said, "I know you Christians worship three gods, but the Bible says that God is one. You all are polytheists!" I tried to reason with him, but all he wanted to do was argue. So, I shifted tactics and began to ask him about his family and his work. He told me a little about his family. and that he owned an art gallery on the east side of Columbus. I told him that that I would love to meet with him sometime, and he became belligerent again. He said, "You Baptists stay out of our area". We don't want you coming over and trying to convert us!" and then he hung up.

There is a growing pressure in our society upon evangelical Christians to back away from this belief that Jesus is the only way to God, and the only entrance into heaven. This appeal is made in the name of tolerance. Some will say, " Why bring Jesus into it?". Why can't we just agree on believing in a supreme being and that there are many ways to know the deity? Well, the reason a Bible believing Christian cannot agree to this is because Jesus and the New Testament do not give us this option. We do not teach that Jesus is the only way because we are bigoted, intolerant or prejudiced against people of other beliefs. No, we believe this and teach it because Jesus Christ, our Lord, commissioned us to take this gospel (Good News) to every people group on the face of the earth. A Christian cannot be faithful to Christ and affirm anything else. This belief and assignment are fundamental to our faith and is rooted in love for all people.

Now this does not justify the behavior of some overzealous Christians who have tried to coerce or manipulate people of other religions or beliefs to receive Christ. Such behavior is inconsistent with His example and instructions. He taught his followers to be sensitive to the leadership of the Holy Spirit and look for open doors He places before us to share our testimony and the gospel. But He and His Apostles clearly commanded His followers to unashamedly proclaim the Good News as truth, but to do it with love and humility.

In proclaiming that Christ is the only way, we are not exalting ourselves above others, but we are exalting Christ as Lord and Savior. We are simply bearing witness to the revealed truth. We are no better than people of other faiths, but we are merely sinners saved by the grace of God. As I said earlier in the chapter on "The Bread of Life", we are like hungry beggars who found bread and we are offering it to others who are also starving.

Objection # 2) Some say that this means that Christianity is narrow minded.

Christians are challenged to be more broadminded. Well, certainly broadmindedness is a good quality if it means to be open to the truth and having a teachable spirit. But on the other hand, once truth is established, truth is very narrow. There is no room for broadmindedness in the chemical laboratory. Water is composed of 2 parts hydrogen and 1 part oxygen. The slightest deviation from this formula is forbidden. There is no room for broadmindedness in music. For example, there can only be eight notes in an octave. The skilled conductor would not permit his first violin to play even so much as one half note off of the written note, chord and key. There is no room for broadmindedness in mathematics. Neither geometry, calculus, nor trigonometry allow any variation from exact accuracy. Even simple additions are very narrow. If 2 plus 2 equals 4, the total cannot at the same time equal 22. But a person is not regarded as being narrow-minded or intolerant if he insists that the only correct answer is 4.

Absolute truth is narrow. Yes, genuine followers of Christ should be tolerant toward people with different points of view and respect their right to be heard. But Christians cannot succumb to the trap of agreeing that all points of view, in the name of tolerance, are equally valid. This is because the Christian view and other world views are mutually exclusive and contradictory. Jesus alone has paid the penalty for our sins when He died on the cross. This is called substitutionary atonement. Jesus alone has been raised from the dead victorious over sin, Satan and death. Jesus alone has ascended, having returned to heaven to intercede on our behalf before the God of Glory, and serves as the mediator between Holy God and repentant humanity who have trusted in Jesus alone for their eternal salvation. And Jesus alone will return a second time at the end this age to establish the Kingdom of Heaven.

Objection #3) Some say this means that Christianity disregards sincerity.

These critics say it doesn't matter what you believe if you are sincere. Their view is that as long as it works for you and gives meaning to your life that is what really counts. What a dangerous position to take! Sincerely believing in something does not make it true. Faith is no more valid than the object in which we place our faith. Sincere faith is no substitute for the truth.

I read a tragic story of a nurse who by mistake put carbolic acid instead of silver nitrate into the eyes of a newborn baby. She was sincere in her effort and motive, but her sincerity did not spare the baby from blindness nor the nurse from the devastating personal consequences that followed.

I recall one time being on vacation, and as I was driving, I was sincere and at peace, until I discovered that somehow, I had missed a turn, and was on the wrong road. This was back in ancient times when there were no such things as GPS or cell phones. So, my sincerity did not spare me from having to pull off the road, get out our big old paper map, unfold it, and figure out how to get back on the right road.

I am sure many of you who are reading these words are familiar with the tragic story of Jim Jones in Guyana. This man had a warped understanding of the Scriptures due to evil desires in his heart. He may have started out with some degree of sincerity, but from the beginning he was so self-absorbed that the evil one (the devil) had taken advantage of his warped mind and gained control and access to his soul.

Jim Jones started out as a Pentecostal preacher who seemed to be sincere on the exterior. He pastored a Pentecostal church in San Francisco called the Peoples Temple between 1955 and 1978. In 1974 he compelled many of the members of his church to follow him to Guyana and live with him there in what was called Jonestown. By 1978 there were reports of abuse of people going on in Jonestown. So, a U.S. congressman named Leo Ryan led a delegation to travel to the commune to observe what was happening. Ryan learned that some members wanted to leave with the congressman. While attempting to board the plane, Ryan and four others were murdered by gunmen from the cult. Jones told the people that this was the end of the age and that it would be best if they all died together. So Jones ordered a mass murder-suicide that resulted in the death of 909 commune members, 304 of them children. They died by drinking Kool-Aid laced with cyanide. Many of the people who followed Jones appeared sincere, but yet naïve and were easily led by a dynamic, and yet demonic personality.

Read this statement carefully; believing in something doesn't make it true anymore than failing to believe truth makes it false. Truth is truth regardless of people's opinions. Facts are facts regardless of people's attitudes. People can be sincere but sincerely wrong. Sincerity is important but alone, it is not enough. In religious matters, the first issue must always be, is it true? Authentic Christians believe that the claims of Christ and the Christian faith can be historically documented as true. We believe that the evidence is beyond reasonable doubt. Sincerity does not replace the necessity of truth.

II. The Alternatives to Christianity

There are a variety of world religions and cults that offer a system of belief significantly different from Christianity. It is helpful to have some familiarity with other religions because it enables us to confirm our own faith as we see the contrasts. It also equips us to be better in our ability to be effective witnesses. So, I want to first make some general observations, and then to look at some examples.

GENERAL OBSERVATIONS

First of all, most religions have some truth mixed with a lot of error. Through God's general revelation in creation, there is truth about God that perceptive people can observe. Look, for example, at what the Apostle Paul wrote in Romans 1:18-20, "For the wrath of God is revealed from heaven against all ungodliness and unrighteousness of men, who by their unrighteousness suppress the truth. For what can be known about God is plain to them, because God has shown it to them. For his invisible attributes, namely, his eternal power and divine nature, have been clearly perceived, ever since the creation of the world, in the things that have been made. So they are without excuse."

Now a degree of moral goodness and wisdom can be found in some non-Christian religions, but there is also much error that is in complete contradiction to God's special revelation found in the Bible and in the person of the Lord Jesus Christ.

Second, nearly all religions are rooted in human effort to know and discover God. They are based on human initiative to know spiritual reality. However, Christianity is the story of God taking the initiative to reveal Himself. Now this is also true of Judaism to a degree, but it

116

doesn't believe that Jesus was God incarnate, which is fundamental to Christianity.

Third, most religions view salvation as a human achievement. They tend to focus on what people must do through their own effort to attain whatever their view of salvation or ultimate reality might be. To use Christian terms, it is a "works" concept of salvation. But Christianity views salvation as a gift from God rooted completely in His grace.

Fourth, most religions have more differences than similarities. There does seem for the most part widespread agreement on what is morally good, but when it comes to comparing systems of belief and worldviews, there are tremendous differences. I say this because some have the mistaken idea that most religions are rather similar and can easily be blended. So, let us look at specific examples.

SPECIFIC EXAMPLES

I have chosen to focus on six of the major world religions. Most of the other religions and cults are offshoots of these I mention below. I am greatly indebted to two authors who have been the primary sources of the information which I share. (Paul Little, "Know Why You Believe" and Fritz Ridenour, "So What's the Difference?")

1. Animism

    This very primitive religion is practiced by aborigines on several continents. Animism believes in a supreme being, but it teaches that this god turned over creation to lesser deities or spirit beings. And so, Animists are constantly trying to placate these spirits who are mostly hostile.

    Animists also believe that the spirits of dead people pass into something else on earth, such as a stone, or a tree, or a crocodile, or even a river. The people of this religion live in constant fear and dread. They are haunted constantly by their fear of the spirit world, and so they worship the dead, as well as multiple spirit beings, to appease them. Black magic and voodooism are also a part of this pagan religion that stirs a sense of dread and horror in the hearts of the worshippers.

2. Hinduism

This religion of India originated in 500 BC. One of its unique characteristics is the caste system. People are divided into various castes based on societal and economic positions, and they do not socialize with people outside of their caste. The lowest caste has no hope of deliverance.

Hinduism is a form of religion called pantheism which says that everything is God and God is everything. This god is called Brahman or the world soul, and only this world soul is real and a part of it dwells within each person. But the rest of the world is an illusion. In other words, it does not really exist. Our body does not exist; pain and death do not exist. The world does not exist for "all is Brahman and Brahman is all".

The goal of the Hindu religion is what its adherents call Nirvana. This experience is compared to a drop of water falling into an ocean. This means that the ultimate hope is to be absorbed by the world soul. In other words, one ceases to have individual consciousness or identity. This process may take thousands of reincarnations. The Hindu believes that as soon as a human, an animal or even an insect dies, he or she or it, is immediately reborn in another form. Whether one moves up or down the scale of life depends on the quality of the moral behavior of the person's previous life.

This process is called the Law of Karma. A good life leads to more comfort and less suffering, whereas an immoral life leads to more suffering and poverty. Another way to understand how the Hindu views the Law of Karma is found in the caste system. A person's goal is to move up the system, but those who live evil lives will end up very low in the system, and maybe even end up as an animal or insect. This is why Hindus will not kill animals or even insects. This has led to serious sanitation and health problems.

3. Buddhism

Unlike the Hindu religion, Buddhism can point to an individual founder. His name is Siddhartha Gautama. He was born a Hindu in India about 560 BC. He would later be called Buddha, which means "enlightened one".

In some ways, Buddhism is like Hinduism from which it evolved. Buddha did accept the Hindu teachings on reincarnation along with Karma. But he denied that humans have a soul which is part of a world soul and he denied that the present world is unreal or an illusion.

Buddha was what we today call an atheist or at least an agnostic. He was more of a philosopher than a religious leader. He decided that the reason people suffer is that they desire things they cannot have, but if they would cease to desire things, then they would not suffer. This is explained in what Buddhists call "Four Noble Truths" which are the following:

1. Suffering is universal

2. The cause of suffering is craving (selfish desire)

3. The cure for suffering is to eliminate desire

4. Desire is eliminated through following the Eightfold Path to Enlightenment. (right knowledge, right feeling, right speech, right action, right living, right effort, right insight and right meditation)

Buddha taught that those who follow this path will eventually experience Nirvana which is total extinction. It has been compared to the snuffing out of a candle. The appeal of this belief is the release from the endless cycle of death and rebirth. Fritz Ridenour writes that "when Buddha was asked to define the state of nirvana, he always said that he never tried to solve this question. His mission was to show man the way to escape the suffering of life, not to describe what he would find once he had been liberated". Paul Little has written the following about reincarnation, "This specifically implies the passing of the 'spark' of life or the soul to become at death some other body or form. Buddha's intent evidently was to help his followers escape the cycle of suffering and desire through birth and rebirth."

4. Confucianism

Confucius was born in China in 557 B.C. He was a wise man who taught many interesting ideas, but like Buddha, he was not attempting to start a religion. In fact, he was an agnostic as far as his own religious persuasion. He taught that man needs no help beyond himself. But his teachings developed into a religion of ethics which begins and ends with man.

Confucius taught piety with regard to relationships, as well as various proverbs on how to live wisely. The Chinese took his teachings and over time blended them with such practices as ancestor worship, animism, and various social traditions, and became known as Confucism or Confucianism.

5. Islam

Islam is a religion that claims 1.8 billion members in the world and dominates 42 nations in Asia, Africa and Europe. And it is spreading rapidly. The word Islam means "submission" (to Allah, the god of Mohammed who founded Islam). The members call themselves Muslims which means "those who submit." Mohammed was born in Arabia in the city of Mecca in AD 570. Mohammed never claimed to be divine, but he did claim to be Allah's greatest prophet. He wrote the Koran which is the sacred book of Islam.

Muslims claim that the present-day Koran was copied from the original which they believe is now in heaven.

The Koran portrays Allah as a god totally removed from the creation. So, to them the idea of an incarnation of Allah is blasphemous. However, they do believe that Allah is the God of Abraham, Moses, the prophets of Israel, and even of Jesus. but they believe that Mohammed is the greatest prophet of all. In fact, the Koran denies that Jesus is the Son of God who died on the cross for the sins of the world and then on the third day arose from the dead.

The Koran teaches that we humans must earn salvation by following the Five Pillars of Islam which are as follows:

First, The Statement of Belief.

> To become a Muslim a person must publicly repeat the creed called Shahadah which says: "There is no god but Allah and Muhammed is the prophet of Allah."

Second, Prayers.

> This is a ritual which must be performed five times a day. This requires a Muslim to kneel and bow in the direction of Mecca, the holy city where Mohammed was born.

Third, the practice of Alms.

> This requires a Muslim to give at least 2.5 % his income as alms for the poor.

Fourth, Ramadan.

> This is the ninth month of the Muslim lunar year which is called Ramadan. This is, for a Muslim, the holiest time of the year. It requires Muslims to fast during the daylight hours for an entire month, but as soon as the sun sets, the feasting begins. But during Ramadan the participant must not commit

any unworthy act. For if he does, then his act of fasting will be considered unacceptable and meaningless.

Fifth, A Pilgrimage to Mecca.

This is called Hajj and is required of every Muslim at least once during their lifetime. If for some reason the pilgrimage is too difficult then someone else can go in their place.

In Islam, heaven is considered a paradise of sensual pleasures, but getting there is achieved ironically by abstaining from such practices while on earth.

Islam also believes in Jihad (Holy War}. This is a religious war through which Islamists use overwhelming force to conquer infidels and spread conflict for the sake of Islam. The use of this kind of force is sanctioned in the Koran. Soldiers who die in such violent deaths are guaranteed entrance into Paradise. This explains why so many Jihadists commit suicide in attempts to kill as many infidels as possible. Now in fairness there are various types of Muslims today who are not militant at all. They are peace-loving moderates.

6. Judaism

Judaism is of course the foundation of Christianity. Devout Jews believe in the same God as Christians do. His name is Yahweh, the God of the Old Testament, who created the universe and first revealed His name to Moses at the burning bush. Yahweh in essence means "I Am". This book which you are reading is based on the claim made by Jesus in John 8:58 where He said, "Truly. Truly, I say to you, before Abraham was, I am." He taught that He was God incarnate and His coming was a fulfillment of the Old Testament prophesies of a coming King and Savior. But those who practice Judaism today do not believe that Jesus is the promised Messiah. Now there are a growing number of Jews today who are professing faith in Jesus as their Lord and Messiah. They call themselves Messianic Jews.

At the heart of Judaism in the Old Testament was its sacrificial system which ended with the destruction of the Temple in Jerusalem (70 AD). As a result, there was no real way to deal with sin and guilt before a Holy God other than try to live a holy life that would be pleasing to God. Now , today, the religion of Judaism exists in three different forms: Orthodox, Conservative and Reform.

Orthodox Jews are still looking for the Messiah and try to follow the letter of the Law. They are very devout in their efforts to study and obey the Torah (or Law) written down by Moses. The Torah are the first five books of the Old Testament and serve as the rule of life for the Orthodox Jew. But Orthodox Jews not only obey the Torah, but they also try to obey other teachings which have been added over the centuries. Some of these teachings were written down around AD 200 in a book called the Mishnah. It consists mostly of instructions for daily living known as the Halakah which means "the way to walk."

The Mishnah is around a thousand pages long, but in AD 500 another holy book was compiled of 36 volumes called the Talmud. It is based on the Mishnah, but much more material was added. This includes famous stories called the Haggadah. These three books (the Torah, the Mishnah, and the Talmud) practically rule every aspect of the lives of Orthodox Jews.

Conservative Jews tend to have a more liberal interpretation of the Torah, but they still believe in its authority. They also want to keep recognizing the authority of the Torah and the traditions of Judaism.

Reform Jews have moved away considerably from Orthodoxy. They teach that the principles of Judaism are more important than the practices. So, most Reform Jews do not observe the dietary laws, nor rules.

But Orthodox, Conservative, and Reform Jews all agree that the Sabbath and the holy days must be at least recognized. Fritz Ridenour in his book titled "So What's the Difference?" quotes an old saying that all three forms of Judaism agree on, which says, "More than Israel kept the Sabbath, the Sabbath kept Israel".

The Old Testament tells us that when the Lord gave the Law to His people through Moses, they were instructed to observe seven annual feasts in the following order. (Much of the following material on the feasts comes from the book titled "The Feasts of the Lord" by Kevin Howard and Marvin Rosenthal.) A Study of these Feasts can be very helpful in equipping Gentile believers in sharing the gospel with our Jewish friends.

1) THE FEAST OF THE PASSOVER is the foundational feast. The six feasts that follow are built upon it. This feast occurs in the Spring of the year on the 14th day of the Hebrew month, Nisan (March/April). After the severe judgment upon Egypt, Pharoah finally relented. What a powerful image which foresaw the Cross, upon which the Son of God would become the Lamb, who would shed his blood as our substitute. He became our sin bearer so that we would be spared from the judgment we deserve. But sadly, today Jews, other than Messianic Jews, do not believe that the Passover pictured the future suffering of Jesus as the Lamb of God. However, this feast does speak of REDEMPTION. Messiah, the Passover Lamb, has been slain for us. He became our substitute, taking upon himself the punishment we deserve.

2) THE FEAST OF UNLEAVENED BREAD. This Feast began the very next day after Passover, on the 15th day of the Hebrew month, Nisan. It was to last for seven days. On the first and seventh nights there was to be a convocation (a meeting time

between God and His people). Now these first two holidays were so closely connected, that with the passing of time, the Jewish people began to observe them as one holiday. It is important to remember that in the Bible, leaven symbolizes sin and death. It is an agent which curses everything and everyone.

But there was one great exception in human history. Jesus, the Messiah, was crucified on Friday and His body was placed in a borrowed tomb which belonged to Joseph of Arimathea. But, unlike all other corpses, there would be no decomposition of His flesh. His body would be exempted from the natural process of decay and corruption. On the day of Pentecost, forty days after the Ascension of Christ, the Holy Spirit was poured out upon the followers of Jesus gathered in Jerusalem. Peter began to preach the Gospel to the masses of people gathered in the city. One of the Messianic passages he quoted was from Psalm 16:10, which said, "For you will not abandon my soul to Hades, or let your Holy One see corruption"

3) THE FEAST OF FIRST FRUITS. This third feast occurred on the second day of the seven-day Feast of Unleavened Bread, on the 16th day of the Hebrew month, Nisan. The barley harvest, the first crop planted in the winter, begins to ripen in the spring. The Lord's acceptance of the first fruits was an earnest or a pledge on His part of a full harvest. Paul was inspired by the Spirit to write the following in 1 Corinthians 15:20-23, "But in fact Christ has been raised from the dead, the firstfruits of those who have fallen asleep. For as by a man came death, by a man has come also the resurrection of the dead. For as in Adam all die, so also in Christ shall all be made alive. But each in his own order: Christ the firstfruits, then at his coming those who belong to Christ."

4) THE FEAST OF WEEKS. This fourth feast is known as Shavuot which is Hebrew for the term "weeks". It is called the Feast of

Weeks because the Lord told the sons of Jacob to count seven weeks from the first fruits and then on the day after this, the fourth feast, the Feast of Weeks was to be observed. Seven weeks are forty-nine days, plus one day after, and this brings the total to fifty. So, the fourth feast was to always occur fifty days after first fruits. This feast was called Pentecost which means "fiftieth". One other instruction for the feast of weeks was that the priests were to each bring two loaves of bread for the fulfillment of the spring feasts.

• The Passover pictures REDEMPTION

Jesus the Messiah became the Passover Lamb for us. He was slain like a lamb that as slaughtered so that believers could be redeemed and set free.

• The Unleavened Bread pictures SANCTIFICATION

To sanctify means to set apart something as holy. The Body of Christ was set apart. God the Father would not allow his body to begin to decay nor begin the process of decomposition during those three days in the grave. On the third day He would emerge from the grave with a glorified resurrected body.

• The First Fruits pictures His RESURRECTION

Jesus, on the third day, after His broken pierced body, which had been wrapped like a mummy and placed in a sealed tomb, emerged from the grave in an incorruptible glorified body and made appearances to over 500 people. The Apostle Paul described the Resurrection in I Corinthians 15:20 "But in fact Christ has been raised from the dead, the first fruits of those who have fallen asleep."

• The Feast of WEEKS

...speaks to the fact that the Lord told the sons of Jacob that they were to count seven weeks from First fruits, and then on the "day after" this, the fourth feast was to be observed and it was called PENTECOST which means "fiftieth."

Now what did this all mean? Well, it all prophetically spoke of the coming of the Holy Spirit which inaugurated the New Covenant and Church Age which the Messiah instituted in the Upper Room. The middle wall of separation between Jews and Gentiles has been broken down by our victorious Lord and Savior who is the Son of God.

This brings us to the three FALL FEASTS:

5) THE FEAST OF TRUMPETS is the first of the feasts in the Fall. The Jewish Community calls this feast ROSH HASHANAH which means "Head of the Year." Now the Scriptures never used this term to designate this specific feast. But rather, it is referred to as Zikhron Teruah ("Memorial of Blowing of trumpets"), Lev 23:24; or Yom Teruah ("Day of Blowing of trumpets"), a day of sounding trumpets in the Temple and throughout the land of Israel. This was observed as the start of the civil year that contrasted with the religious year which started right before Passover.

Now the blowing of trumpets in ancient Israel served two basic purposes: The first was to call God's people to a solemn assembly. The was for the purpose of assembling the children of Israel together into the Holy presence of Yahweh to receive specific instructions and pray about a matter of grave importance. A second reason was to receive divine direction to go to war. The trumpets were called shofars which were in realty ram's horns.

Many also see this feast as corresponding with the present age. The last of the Spring feasts celebrate PENTECOST which represents the outpouring of the Holy Spirit and the birth of the Church age, and then in the Fall there is the Feast of the Trumpets which infers to many the Rapture of the Church.

6) The SECOND of the Fall annual feasts is called THE DAY OF ATONEMENT and takes place ten days from the Trumpets. These ten days are also known as the Days of Awe. This event was intended to be a solemn occasion for self-examination and prayers of repentance. This feast was fulfilled from a Christian perspective when Jesus died on the Cross of Calvary. Christians view this as the ultimate and final sacrifice for the sins of humanity. Romans 5:8-9, "But God shows His love for us in that while we were still sinners, Christ died for us. Since, therefore, we have now been justified by His blood, much more shall we be saved by Him from the wrath of God."

7) The THIRD and final annual feast during the Fall, which lasts seven days, is called THE FEAST OF TABERNACLES, and it usually occurs in October. Devout Jews erect small "booths" or "huts" made from bullrushes as a reminder of the temporary huts their forefathers built during the Exodus wanderings in the wilderness. Portions of the Fall crop are hung in the booth of each family as a way of acknowledging God's faithfulness to provide for His chosen people.

I mentioned earlier in this book a very significant event related to the Feast of Tabernacles which John records in His Gospel. Let's revisit it again. In John's Gospel 7:37-38," On the last day of the feast, the great day, Jesus. stood up and cried out, "If anyone thirsts, let him come to me and drink. Whoever believes in me, as the scripture has said, 'Out of his heart will flow rivers of living water'."

I love what Warren Wiersbe wrote in his Commentary on the New Testament about this section. To paraphrase, he in essence said, 'that the last day of the feast was the seventh day. This day was a very special event during which the priests would march around the altar seven times, chanting Psalm 118:25, "Save us, we pray, O Lord! O Lord. We pray, give us success!" It would be the last day they would draw the water and pour it out. The pouring out of the water most likely was symbolic of the water Moses drew from the rock. Jesus stood and shouted His great invitation to thirsty sinners (John 7:37-38). Jesus was making it as clear as possible that His Spirit alone was the source of life and blessing that can meet the need of every human heart who believes.

Well, this gives us an overview. What do you think? When I personally compare authentic Biblical Christianity to what other world religions and philosophies offer, I choose Jesus!!! I have chosen to close this study with a focus on five distinctives which convince me that Christianity is true, and has the greatest appeal for me intellectually, emotionally and practically.

III. The Appeal of Christianity

A. THE INCARNATION

The word incarnate means "in flesh". In Christian doctrine, the incarnation refers to the clear teaching in the New Testament that God the Son visited this earth as a man. Other world religions are really the efforts of humanity to know the divine or at least discover ultimate truth. But the finite cannot penetrate the infinite. However, Christianity is the authentic story of the infinite penetrating the finite. God has visited this planet as a perfect man, and His name is Jesus.

Look again at the Gospel of John 1:1, "In the beginning was the Word, and the Word was with God, and the Word was God... 1:14a,"and the Word became flesh and dwelt among us, and we have seen His glory". So, John proceeded to make clear that the Word made flesh was Jesus. Remember later in John's Gospel, Philip asked Jesus to reveal to them the Father, and Jesus said in

129

response, "Have I been with you so long, and yet you have not known Me, Philip? He who has seen me has seen the Father, so how can you say,' Show us the Father'?" Of all the most prominent religious leaders who founded world religions, only Jesus claimed to be the personal God who created the universe. The emphasis of other world religions is not to worship the leader, but rather to follow his teachings. But this is not so with Jesus. He made Himself the focal point of His teaching.

We read in Matthew 16:13 that Jesus led his disciples far north of Galilee into Gentile territory called Caesarea Philippi. They were about 120 miles north of Jerusalem. This area had historically been identified with various pagan religions. It had been a stronghold for Baal worship. The false Greek god Pan had shrines there, and there was also a temple built there to honor Caesar Augustus.

It was in the midst of this pagan setting that Jesus asked His disciples two questions: The first was, "Who do people say that the Son of Man is?" Their response was, John the Baptist, Elijah, Jeremiah, or one of the other prophets.

The second question was more direct and personal; He said to them, "but who do you say that I am?" Simon Peter replied, "You are the Christ, the Son of the Living God." Jesus answered and said to him, "Blessed are you, Simon Bar-Jonah! For flesh and blood has not revealed this to you, but my Father who is in heaven."

Of all the leaders who founded the largest world religions, only Jesus claimed to be the personal God who created the universe. The emphasis of other world religions is not so much to worship their leader, but rather to follow his teachings. But not so with Jesus; He made Himself the focal point of His teachings.

This does not make the teachings of Jesus insignificant, but rather His identity lends a heaviness and a much greater sense of accountability to Him. However, the highest motivation for obeying

Him is not rooted in fearful horror, but rather in a sense of respect, appreciation and great affection for our Lord who loves us this much.

B. THE ATONEMENT

Atonement refers to being reconciled to God through having our sins judged and forgiven. The other religions of the world have no real solution to the sin problem. In fact, some simply ignore it. For example, Hinduism and Buddhism teach that the real problem is suffering, but Judaism and Christianity are realistic and face the problem of sin. The Old Testament describes the rebellion of humanity against God, but the Jewish prophets, inspired by God's Spirit, foresaw a day when God would intervene in human history and send the Messiah (Anointed One) to confront our sinful condition and voluntarily lay down his life by taking upon Himself the judgment we deserve.

The Messiah would make an atoning sacrifice for our sins. Atonement refers to being reconciled to God. In this study we have already focused on how the New Testament gives us historical accounts of this promised Messiah named Jesus of Nazareth, documenting the fulfillment in detail of how Jesus was born of a virgin, lived a perfect life, performed signs and wonders, astounded people with the authority and power of His teaching and miracles, was arrested and falsely accused, was crucified, buried in a sealed tomb and yet was raised from the dead on the third day, making at least ten appearances over a period of forty days to more than 500 eyewitnesses.

So, the Good News is that God has intervened in history out of His great love for us rebellious creatures. John 3:16 says, "For God so loved the world, that He gave HIS only Son, that whoever believes in Him should not perish but have eternal life." Romans 5:8 says, "but God shows His love for us in that while we were still sinners, Christ died for us."

C. THE RESURRECTION

None of these other World Religions claim to have a resurrected Savior, but Christianity does. Jesus Christ arose from the dead, leaving behind an empty tomb, and appearing to over 500 eyewitnesses. All other founders or leaders of various religions in the world died, never to be heard from again. But all four of the gospel accounts give us various testimonies from those who saw and even communicated with the risen Lord after the Romans officially declared that Jesus was dead.

John the Apostle, who was a follower of Jesus for three years prior to our Lord's crucifixion, closed his own gospel story by describing an amazing encounter he, along with some of the other disciples, had with the risen Lord. Peter decided to go fishing and six of the other disciples, including John, decided to join him. They fished all night and caught nothing. When morning arrived, Jesus stood on the shore, but they did not recognize Him at first. Possibly the morning fog and mist in the air hindered their vision. But then Jesus said to them, "Children, do you have any fish?", They replied to him with a straightforward answer of "No." Jesus responded by saying, "Cast the net on the right side of the boat, and you will find some." They obeyed, and the result was such a large haul of fish, the disciples were barely able to pull it in.

In that moment John immediately recognized that it was Jesus, and he proclaimed to Peter, "It is the Lord!" Oh, Wonder of Wonders! The only begotten Son of God has visited this planet as one of us! He came to do for us what we could never do for ourselves. He came to die for our sins as a substitute for sinners, He was buried in a tomb, but on the third day He arose from the dead, leaving behind an empty tomb, as well as empty graves clothes. Over a period of forty days, He made at least ten appearances to over five hundred eyewitnesses. His disciples who at first were filled with doubt and anxiety, were transformed into courageous followers who would all die as martyrs except for John. He would be banished to an island called Patmos, where he would experience an incredible encounter with the risen Lord. This encounter resulted in the book of Revelation, the last book in the Bible.

D. SALVATION BY GRACE THROUGH FAITH.

Every other religious system is essentially a "do-it-yourself" proposition. In other words, religion says "follow these teachings"; "measure up these principles"; or "meet these rules and requirements" and "you, through your good effort, will earn God's favor and achieve salvation." The problem, of course, is that we humans are fallen creatures and therefore we have a predisposition to sin, and in our fallen state we are utterly incapable of saving ourselves. Romans 3:10, 23 says: "None is righteous, no, not one.....for all have sinned and fall short of the glory of God".

This is why we all desperately need grace. And this is what Christianity offers every sinner who repents (in genuine remorse turning away from a life of sin that separates this person from God) and trusts in Jesus alone as his/her Lord and Savior and by faith receives from Him the glorious gift of eternal life. You see, grace is being given as a wonderful gift which you have not earned nor merited.

So, the Good News is that we do not need to labor nor try to earn God's favor. He simply calls upon us to repent and believe in Jesus. There Is no real assurance or hope in other religions. It's like giving a set of swimming instructions to a man who is already in the process of drowning. But Jesus is our lifeguard who jumps into the water and rescues us. Ephesians 2:8-9 says, "For by grace you have been saved through faith. And this is not of your own doing; it is the gift of God".

E. GLORIFICATION

This is the term which refers to our final state in eternity as believers in Jesus. Earlier I referenced Romans 3:23, which says that all sinners have fallen short of the glory of God, but someday we will no longer fall short of His glory. Romans 8:30 says, 'And those whom He predestined He also called, and those whom He called, He also justified, and those whom He justified He also glorified." As I alluded to earlier, to be glorified means to be delivered from all the effects of sin and be made perfect in body, soul and spirit. This does not mean extinction nor a loss of identity. It means that you will become a perfect version of you.

We will live in perfect fellowship with the Father, the Son and the Holy Spirit forevermore. We will have a new glorified body, like Jesus' body, living in a new creation where there will no more sin nor death nor suffering ever again.

I have chosen to close with two amazing promises to every sincere believer in Jesus as your Lord and Savior.

Philippians 3:20-21, "But our citizenship is in heaven, and from it we await a Savior, the Lord Jesus Christ, who will transform our lowly body to be like His glorious body, by the power that enables Him even to subject all things to Himself."

John 3:2, "Beloved, we are God's children now, and what we will be has not yet appeared, but we know that when He appears we shall be like him, because we shall see Him as He is."

Seven

"I Am the True Vine"

JOHN 15:1-11, 16: "I am the true vine, and my father is the vinedresser. Every branch in me that does not bear fruit he takes away, and every branch that does bear fruit he prunes, that it may bear more fruit. Already you are clean because of the word that I have spoken to you. Abide in me, and I in you. As the branch cannot bear fruit by itself, unless it abides in the vine, neither can you, unless you abide in me. I am the vine; you are the branches. Whoever abides in me and I in him, he it is that bears much fruit, for apart from me you can do nothing. If anyone does not abide in me he is thrown away like a branch and withers; and the branches are gathered, thrown into the fire, and burned. If you abide in me, and my words abide in you, ask whatever you wish, and it will be done for you. By this my Father is glorified, that you bear much fruit and so prove to be my disciples. As the Father has loved me, so have I loved you. Abide in my love. If you keep my commandments, you will abide in my love, just as I have kept my Father's commandments and abide in his love. These things I have spoken to you, that my joy may be in you, and that your joy may be full.

You did not choose me, but I chose you and appointed you that you should go and bear fruit and that your fruit should abide, so that whatever you ask the Father in my name, he may give it to you."

The great missionary, Hudson Taylor, told of a time in his life when he was really struggling spiritually. As he tried his best to live for Christ and serve Him in ministry, Taylor felt an overwhelming sense of weakness and distress. God used another missionary named John McCarthy to open the eyes of Hudson Taylor's heart to a new perspective on Christian living.

McCarthy wrote a letter that the Lord used to transform Taylor's life. McCarthy's letter was based on the lesson Jesus taught His disciples about the relationship between a vine and its branches. McCarthy pointed out that a branch does not struggle and strain to bear fruit. It simply remains (abides) in the vine, because it's the vine that does all the work. In other words, the fruit is a product of the sap that runs through the vine into the branch. Taylor realized he had been striving to produce spiritual fruit through his own dedicated energy rather than allowing the True Vine (the Lord Jesus) to produce fruit through him. So, Hudson Taylor said that he learned that the Christian Life is a life of abiding in Christ as a branch abides in a vine. This does not mean that we are to be passive, as I will point out later in this chapter, but this is the starting point for living a productive life for the glory of our Lord.

This last chapter concludes our study of the seven I AM sayings recorded in the gospel of John. The final two "I Am" sayings spoken by Christ were a part of a sermon (or lesson) that runs from John 13 through 17. He began His message in the Upper Room. After washing the feet of His disciples, observing the Lord's Supper, and the exit of Judas, Jesus made perhaps the most controversial statement of His ministry. It is the sixth "I AM" saying from John 14:6 where Jesus said, "I am the way, the truth, and the life. No one comes to the Father except through me". The exclusivity of this statement offended many in the first century and continues to do so today. But as we studied in the previous chapter, absolute truth is always exclusive. This is also true of the final and seventh "I am" saying of Jesus in this setting.

When God the Son came to this earth, as a man, the Father's preordained plan was never for His Son to remain here in His bodily presence. As I have repeatedly said throughout this study, Jesus came, first of all, through His teaching, to proclaim the good news of the Kingdom; to confront the darkness of our fallen world; to perform signs and wonders as evidence of His identity; to call Jewish people as well as Gentiles to repentance and faith in Him as the promised Messiah; to demonstrate through word and deed the mercy and compassion of a loving God; as well as a severe judgment upon those who have hardened their hearts against God and refuse to repent and believe. But the primary reason Jesus, the Son of God, came to this earth was never for Him to remain here in His bodily presence. He came, of course, to identify with us and do for us what we could never have done for ourselves. He voluntarily chose to die on a cruel cross for our sins, be raised from the dead by the Heavenly Father and the Holy Spirit, having conquered sin, death and the devil, and then ascended back to heaven as the victor, and serve as the bridge between God and repentant sinners.

As the time of His departure drew near, He began to prepare His disciples. At this point, He had gathered the disciples in the Upper Room. In John 14 we read where He repeatedly alluded to the fact that He must go away. Now the thought of continuing without Him no doubt aroused both sadness and fear in their hearts. I am sure that they struggled to grasp how things would and could work out, if indeed He was about to leave them.

And so, as He moved toward His final hours on this planet, He used the metaphor of the vine and branches, to explain the nature of their future relationship with Him. So in this chapter, I invite you to join me as we examine the powerful picture our Lord has given to us.

As we read the words of our Lord, the symbolism is very clear:

- The VINE represents CHRIST. (verses 1,5)

- The BRANCHES represent individual believers or the CHURCH. (verse 5)

- The VINEDRESSER represents GOD the FATHER (the Gardener). (verse 1)

I. OUR POSITION IN CHRIST

The New Testament clearly teaches that the moment we receive Christ as Lord and Savior a miracle occurs. We experience a divine connection. Through placing our faith in Christ, we enter a spiritual union with Him. You see, Christ gives us more than His teaching or a good example to follow. He gives us himself. When we receive Him by faith a miracle occurs. We are united with Him. Now, obviously, this does not mean that we become Christ. We remain separate in personhood and identity, but we are spiritually linked to Him.

The metaphor of the vine and branches beautifully illustrates the nature of this connection. It pictures the miracle of our spiritual position in Christ. Those who have truly experienced what Jesus called being born of the Spirit have an ongoing consciousness of His Spirit prompting, convicting, convincing and comforting us. But we must be open and receptive to what the Old Testament prophet Elijah described as a "still, small voice".

And so, those who are authentic believers will experience this position in Christ in two ways (as a branch is in a vine). The apostle Paul used the phrase "in Christ" or "in Christ Jesus" 82 times in his New Testament letters. When such parallel terms as "in the beloved", "in the Lord" or "in Him" are included, the total amounts to 172 times.

A. **WE ARE IN CHRIST.** (As a branch is in a vine). A study of how the Holy Spirit inspired Paul to use these phrases reveals two concepts about being in Christ:

FIRST, WE ARE UNITED WITH CHRIST IN HIS STANDING BEFORE GOD THE FATHER. To be in Christ means that we are in solidarity with Christ before the Father relationally and legally. According to the New Testament, right now, where is the visible bodily presence of Christ? He is in Heaven enthroned as Lord at the right hand of the Father. This is the position of ultimate power and authority, but also a position of accessibility and acceptance. Note what Paul wrote in Ephesians 2:4-6, "But God, being rich in mercy, because of the great love with which He loved us, even when we were dead in our trespasses, made us alive together with Christ—by grace you have been saved—and raised us up with Him and seated us with Him in the heavenly places in Christ Jesus."

And so, since we are spiritually linked with Christ in solidarity, then in a sense, we are seated with Him in Heaven. He represents us there, and so, as believers, our spiritual position is right before the throne of God, in Christ. This means that as the Father looks at us as believers, He sees us in Christ. This is the power of the gospel. In Christ, we have been declared righteous before a Holy God. We have been justified, and are at peace with God, therefore we have complete access to God anytime, under any circumstances. Note this amazing statement by the apostle Paul in Romans 5:1-2, "Therefore, since we have been justified by faith, we have peace with God through our Lord Jesus Christ. Through him we have also obtained access by faith into this grace in which we stand, and we rejoice in the hope of the glory of God."

And so, we share in Christ's victory, power and authority. All that the Father has given to Christ His Son is also ours to enjoy. The

New Testament teaches that we are joint heirs with Christ, and He has given us the right to use His name, if we use it in a way that is consistent with His character and purpose. Some have compared it to being given a "Power of Attorney". This means to be given delegated legal authority to transact business in the name of another person. There is a sense in which when we pray in the name of Jesus, we are praying for His will to be done.

SECOND, WE ARE IN CHRIST, AS OUR SOURCE FOR SPIRITUAL LIFE. To receive Christ as Lord and Savior involves a spiritual transformation. Prior to our conversion, in our natural state as sinners, we were spiritually dead in our trespasses and sins, separated from God. But when we are saved, we experience a spiritual regeneration. Note Paul's description in 2 Corinthians 5:17, "Therefore, if anyone is in Christ, he is a new creation, old things have passed away, behold all things have become new". Jesus called this being "born again" during His conversation in John 3 with Nicodemus. Just at the life of the vine (or sap) flows through the vine into the branches it is also true that the Spirit of the indwelling Christ enables us to experience His transforming life-giving power within our souls.

In our natural state as sinners we have all been far away from God, living lives ruled by the world, the flesh and the devil, but then we met the Master, and we were transformed into a new people. Not a perfect people, but a new people, empowered by the risen Lord (the Vine).

And this is because, not only are we in Christ, but...

B. **CHRIST IS IN US.**

Yes, His bodily presence is in Heaven, but remember that Christ, as God the Son, has all of the attributes of God the Father and God the Holy Spirit. This means that He is also omnipresent, and so through the Holy Spirit, Christ resides within each believer. He indwells us at the moment of our conversion and promises that He will always be with us. Note the Apostle Paul's words in 2 Corinthians 13:5b, "do you not realize this about yourselves, that Jesus Christ is in you?"; also in Colossians 1:27, "To them God chose to make known how great among the Gentiles are the riches of the glory of this mystery, which is Christ in you, the hope of glory"; Galatians 2;20; "I have been crucified with Christ. It is no longer I who live, but Christ who lives in me. And the life I now live in the flesh I live by faith in the Son of God, who loved me and gave Himself for me"; Romans 8:9-10; 'You, however, are not in the flesh but in the Spirit, if in fact the Spirit of God dwells in you. Anyone who does not have the Spirit of Christ does not belong to him. But if Christ is in you, although the body is dead because of sin, the Spirit is life because of righteousness."

I will never forget the impact it had upon me as a young man when I began to understand this incredible truth. Dr. Ray Edmund, as well as others, have called this "the exchanged life". I live, yet not I, but Christ lives in me. I have chosen to exchange my life for His. So, this means that our spiritual position, as branches, means that we are in Christ and Christ is in us. This may sound like a contradiction, but it isn't when one thinks it through. These two concepts complement each other. We dwell in Him as the part does in the whole, as the branch does in the vine, receiving its life and energy. And in turn, He dwells in us as the whole does in the part, as the vine dwells in the branch sending forth its life and energy to every part.

What a glorious position we have in our relationship to Christ. This is what makes living the Christian life so meaningful and thrilling. This is what enables a local church to have an impact in the community and beyond. None of us will be perfect, but through the grace of our Lord He can take little twigs and enable us to flourish for His Glory. Oh, don't miss this incredible truth. Only one person can live a perfect life and that person is of course our Lord and Savior. This is why Jesus said what He did in verse 5, "I am the vine; you are the branches. Whoever abides in me and I in him, he it is that bears much fruit, for apart from me you can do nothing," Obviously, a branch that is not connected to the vine has no life, and it is unable to produce fruit and so it is with a person who is not connected to Christ. But this raises a question about what are we supposed to do in a practical sense as branches on the vine? What kind of fruit does our Vine want us to produce?

II. OUR PURPOSE IN CHRIST

Let's look once again at our Savior's instruction in John 15:1-2,"I am the true vine, and my Father is the vinedresser. Every branch in me that does not bear fruit he takes away, and every branch in me that does bear fruit he prunes, that it may bear more fruit"; John 15:6, "If anyone does not abide in me he is thrown away like a branch and withers; and the branches are gathered, thrown into the fire and burned"; John 15:16, "You did not choose me, but I chose you and appointed you that you that you should go and bear fruit, and that your fruit should abide…" The obvious point Jesus made is that the purpose of a branch on a grapevine is to produce grapes, or as Jesus said, "to bear fruit." The vinedresser prunes the branches to enable them to bear even more fruit. Those branches which bear no fruit are considered useless and are cut off. Likewise, Christ the Vine expects us believers, His branches, to bear fruit.

Notice that Christ did not expect His branches to create fruit, but simply to bear it. Furthermore, He did not expect the branches to produce *some*, but rather *much* fruit. Those branches which bear no fruit, I believe represent those who profess to believe in Christ, but do not possess genuine saving faith. They are pretenders and are removed from the vine.

But why does our Lord want us to bear much fruit? Notice again what Jesus said in verse eight. "By this my Father is glorified, that you bear much fruit and so prove to be my disciples". I have emphasized in this book that the purpose for our existence is to glorify God. This is proof that we are genuine disciples of Christ. But what does it mean to

142

glorify God? Well, it certainly does not mean that we can somehow make God more glorious. We cannot add to nor enhance His glory. This would be like us humans trying to enhance the brilliant glory of the sun, but we can be like the moon. The moon reflects the brilliant light of the sun, but it certainly is far less in its brilliance. And so, it is with us. Through our character and actions, we can reflect His glory and make it known. We can do this by bearing fruit. But what is fruitfulness? Or, what is the fruit that we should bear? I believe that the New Testament reveals at least four kinds of spiritual fruit that we should bear.

1. The Fruit of a Christian Witness

Notice a Spirit-inspired remark which Paul made in his introduction to the letter he wrote to the Roman church in the first chapter, verse 13 (NKJV). He wrote, "Now I do not want you to be unaware brethren, that I often planned to come to you (but I was hindered until now), that I might have FRUIT among you also, just as among the other Gentiles." The ESV translates the word for "fruit" as "harvest." He was obviously speaking of fruit as new converts to Christ.

Jesus, before He returned to glory, commissioned His disciples to go forth into every nation on earth as His witnesses and make disciples. This means that even to this very day we are called to reproduce ourselves as followers of Christ. The fruit that we bear, if authentic, will have seed in it for more fruit. This results in more and more fruit, or more and more disciples, and this glorifies God. Warren Wiersbe has pointed out that there is a big difference between "results" and "fruit". It is possible to get results statistically but not bear much fruit. D L Moody, the great evangelist, encountered a drunk on the street, who said with slurred speech, "Mr. Moody, I am one of your converts". Moody replied, "You must be one of mine, you don't appear to be one of the Lords." (From Lyle W, Dorsett's biography of D.L. Moody titled, "A Passion For Souls")

2. The Fruit of Christian Works

Notice in Colossians 1:10 how Paul prayed that the Colossian church members would be "fruitful in every good work". Now the good works to which Paul refers are good deeds of service and ministry done in the name of Christ for the glory of God. These are typically acts of Christlike love and mercy. Notice Paul's inspired words in Ephesians 2:10, "For we are His workmanship, created in Christ Jesus for good works, which God prepared beforehand, that we should walk in them." Let us not forget Matthew 5:16 where Jesus says, "In the same way, let your light shine before others, so that they may see your good works and give glory to your Father who is in heaven."

The Apostle Paul would sometimes refer to giving our money to help needy people as fruit. When you think about it, what does a branch do? It gives. If it is living, it is giving. A branch does not bear fruit for its own nourishment, but for the nourishment for others. What a beautiful picture that should inspire all of us!

3. The Fruit of Christian Worship.

Look at Hebrews 13:15, "Through him then let us continually offer up a sacrifice of praise to God, that is, the fruit of lips that acknowledge his name." The Old Testament worshiper brought the fruit of his field as a thanks offering to God. The New Testament worshipers first bring the fruit of their lips. By our words we praise and glorify God. With our lips, we sing; we pray; we confess; we testify; we teach; we edify; and we preach.

I view preaching as an act of worship. I was greatly impacted by Warren Wiersbe's book titled "Real Worship". Dr. Wiersbe wrote, "If preaching is not an act of worship, then the church will end up worshiping the preacher and what he says rather than worshiping God." The great reformer Martin Luther once said, "When I declare the Word of God, I offer sacrifice; When thou hearest the Word of God with all thy heart, thou dost offer sacrifice".

Our worship of God with our lips should include not only preaching, but also testimonies; reading the scriptures; singing hymns and praise choruses; special music presentations; observance of the ordinances (baptisms and the Lords Supper); responsive scripture readings, and verbal affirmations. But it should not be chaotic, which was a problem at the church in Corinth. Paul addressed this problem in I Corinthians 14, concluding his instructions with verse 40 which says. "But all things should be done decently and in order."

Our worship of God with our lips should be natural for us. We are simply bearing fruit as a result of our connection to Christ the Vine who flows in and through our lives.

4. The Fruit of a Christian Walk

A Christian walk is a lifestyle rooted in the indwelling power of the Holy Spirit. It is described in Galatians 5:16 which says, "But I say, walk by (or in) the Spirit and you will not gratify the desires of the flesh (our fallen nature)." The term "walk" describes an ongoing way of life or a lifestyle. So, to walk in the Spirit means an ongoing lifestyle empowered by the Holy Spirit/or the Spirit of Christ. What happens when we walk in the Spirit? Notice what it says later in the same chapter in verses 22-23 where Paul lists nine character traits which he describes as fruit of the Spirit. These traits are love, joy, peace, patience, kindness, goodness, faithfulness, gentleness. and self-control. Now these are character traits which describe the character of Christ himself, who is the Vine.

So a fruitful Christ follower is a person who day by day, chooses to yield to the indwelling Spirit, inviting Him to manifest the character of Christ, our Vine, through his/her life. We need to constantly remind ourselves that the end goal for our lives according to Romans 8:29 is that we be conformed to the image of Christ.

We need to keep in mind a couple of truths about the Fruit of the Spirit: First, these character traits are developed as a unified cluster in each believer. Notice that in this Galatians passage Paul does not refer to the "fruits" of the Spirit, but it is singular (fruit).

Our youngest child Kevin worked in the produce department for a couple of grocery chains. It is interesting to watch how people choose their fruit as they examine their apples, bananas, melons, oranges. etc. Some people are rushed and will pick out their fruit after a quick examination, but others will invest a considerable amount of time looking for the perfect produce. They will pick them up and squeeze them, thump them and closely examine them for any flaws and then finally make their choices.

But it doesn't work this way when we receive the Fruit of the Spirit. We don't pick and choose qualities we think best fit our personalities. We need to memorize Romans 8:29, which says that those whom God foreknew he also predestined to be conformed to the image of His Son. Now keep in mind a couple of truths about the fruit of the Spirit. First, it is not that we pick and choose which qualities we would most like to express. This is not how it works. But the Lord intends to produce all these Christlike qualities in and through our lives for His glory as we continue to grow spiritually in the Vine. The fruit of the Vine takes time to mature, and likewise this is true of as believers. As we continue to mature, we as believers will more and more consistently bear the fruit of the Spirit. But how does this happen? This leads us to a third basic observation about our connection to Jesus as the Vine.

III. OUR POWER FROM CHRIST

I read the story about a little boy who was disappointed with the small size of the eggs that his hen laid. So one day, he hopped on his bike and rode it to the center of the small farming community and returned with a large package. He knelt in front of his hen, unwrapped the package and revealed a large ostrich egg. He held it before his hen and said, "Now, take a good look at this and TRY HARDER!"

This is the way it is with a lot of us Christians. We are often inclined to try to produce Christlike fruit through our own willpower and ability. And when we fail, we just try harder and end up frustrated, filled with guilt and doubt. But, as I have already emphasized, bearing spiritual fruit that glorifies God is not something we can do through our own effort alone. But because of our position in Christ, we have access to an unlimited power source.

The life of Christ, through the Holy Spirit, enables us to fulfill God's purpose. But we must remember that there is a clear distinction between the Vine and the Branches. The two are joined but not equal. But the common denominator in nature is the sap, likewise the common denominator for believers in Christ, is the Holy Spirit. The sap is the life of the vine as it flows into the branches, and so it is with those who have trusted in Christ as Lord and Savior. When we received Jesus into our lives, His omnipresent Spirit literally came to indwell each believer. Jesus describes it as being "born again" of the Spirit. He describes this miracle during his conversation with Nicodemus in the gospel of John, chapter three.

Once a person has experienced this new birth, as they grow and learn, that person begins to be much more conscious of the presence of God empowering, convicting, prompting, instructing and leading through what has been described as a "still, small voice" (or a quiet inner prompting).

So, as the branch draws life from the vine in order to produce fruit, likewise, so must we draw life from a dependency upon Christ our Vine. But there are some basic principles we must put into practice to fully experience this power from our Lord.

1. We Must Abandon Ourselves to His Purpose.

By choosing the word 'abandon', I mean we must choose to let go of a self-centered life and commit to be a fully devoted follower of Christ. Jesus said in Luke 9:23, "If anyone desires to come after me, let him deny himself and take up his cross daily and follow me." The Apostle Paul wrote a letter to Christ followers in Rome in which he said in Romans 12:1, "I appeal to you therefore, brothers, by the mercies of God, to present your bodies as a living sacrifice, holy and acceptable to God, which is your spiritual worship."

We have seen in Verse 8 that our Lord's purpose is for us to bear fruit for the glory of God and not for ourselves. This means that we must not only abandon a self-centered life, but willfully choose a Christ-centered life, or as we follow the metaphor, a vine-centered life.

First of all, this requires DEPENDENCE.

Notice once again the last phrase of verse 5 which says, "without me you can do nothing". We must fully and completely trust in Christ alone. We must totally rely upon His divine enablement. Take note of the incredible promise that the Spirit of God inspired Paul to write in Philippians 2:12b-13, "...work out your own salvation with fear and trembling, for it is God who works in you, both to will and to work for his good pleasure". Notice Paul writes that God works in us and gives us both the desire and the ability to do what pleases Him. So, there must be our best effort, but this effort is dependent upon the strength and power of the Spirit of Christ in us. This calls for the abandonment of self-trust and the surrender of faith. But not only does this kind of power require dependence and a sense of humility.

Second, this requires OBEDIENCE.

For example, the "Fruit of the Spirit" is most definitely the work of the Spirit and not of the flesh. But this does not mean that we bear fruit passively without human effort. Every one of the nine character traits listed as "Fruit of the Spirit" are also commanded in the scriptures to be practiced as acts of obedience. Let us focus on the first three fruits listed by Paul (love, joy and peace).

The first fruit of the Spirit is "love". In Matthew 22:34-40 we find a familiar passage where the Pharisees gathered around Jesus and his disciples. One of their lawyers asked a question designed to test Jesus. So, he asked the Lord this question, "Teacher, which is the greatest commandment in the Law?" Jesus responded with the following answer: "You shall love the Lord your God with all your heart and with all your soul and with all your mind. This is the first and great commandment. And the second is like it: You shall love your neighbor as yourself. On these two commandments rest all the Law and the Prophets." This makes it clear that love is not something that we do automatically, but it is a choice, that as we step out in faith, the Holy Spirit will give us the desire and the ability to do it.

Let us look at the second fruit which is "joy". Joy certainly involves our human emotions, but it is also something we choose to do as an act of faith. For example, the Apostle Paul wrote the Philippian Church during a tough time in his ministry. He was in prison, chained to a Roman soldier, facing the possibility of execution. But despite his circumstances, his letter is filled with so much joy, many have referred to it as "the epistle of joy". I am certain that Paul did not emotionally feel like rejoicing, but he did it by faith. And faith is not an emotion, it is an act of the will rooted in a complete trust in the living God. For example, in Philippians 4:4 Paul wrote, "Rejoice in the Lord always; again, I will say, rejoice."

The third fruit mentioned is "peace". Once again peace is a deep sense of well-being whatever the outward circumstances may be. There is a peace with God which means we have been reconciled to Him, but there is also the peace of God. This refers to an inner serenity or contentment. An example from nature can be helpful; try to imagine a huge storm raging on the surface of a vast ocean. Large waves are tossing and churning. But deep beneath the surface there is very little disturbance. In the depths of the ocean there is a complete calmness. This pictures the peace of God which He will give us as we choose by faith to rely upon the indwelling Spirit of God rather than upon the weakness of our flesh.

Keep in perspective that these commands are directed to the human will. The Lord supplies spiritual power, but we must choose to act in faith and cooperate. It is somewhat like using a tool empowered by electricity. We actively use the tool, but the tool only works when connected to electrical power. This means that we must abandon a dependence on self, but fully trust and obey the Lord in order to bear much fruit for the glory of God.

In the mid-eighteen hundreds, a young man named Dwight L Moody heard a British evangelist Henry Varley say, " It remains for the world to see what the Lord can do with a man wholly consecrated to Christ". This idea took a powerful hold upon Moody. He could not get it out of his mind. Moody contemplated this idea for several weeks. It had so captured his heart that one day he declared, "By the Holy Spirit in me, I will be that man." And that man, D. L. Moody, would impact two continents for Christ! Most historians consider him to be the greatest evangelist of the nineteenth century. Let us move on to consider a second key to experiencing the power of Christ. Not only must we abandon to His purpose, but secondly:

2. We Must Abide in His Presence.

Notice in these verses in John 15 how often Christ emphasizes that our fruitfulness depends on us abiding in Him as the Vine. Look at verses 4-7. What does it mean to abide in the vine? The word "abide" means to (remain). So, when a person gets baptized it pictures the fact that a person has in a sense agreed to die to the old life without Christ and is raised up a new creation in Christ. But this new person is like a new branch connected to Christ as our Vine. What does it mean to abide in Him? And how do we abide in Him?

* This includes REMAINING IN HIM

The Greek word translated "abide" can also be translated as remain, continue, or dwell. It is also similar to the word "abode", which is a noun and has the same root. In John 15, the word "abide" is used by Christ in the continual present tense. And so, it means to keep on remaining in Christ. It means to maintain an unbroken connection. This clearly implies the necessity of a constant, active, relationship with Christ. We should do this not for the purpose of keeping ourselves saved, but in order to live a fruitful life for the glory of almighty God. We are already secure in His grip.

I love the phrase popularized by Brother Lawrence years ago which is "Practicing the Presence of God". All through each day, maintain a consciousness of His presence. Periodically, in your mind worship Him; fellowship with Him; express to Him your gratitude for His blessings and abide in His love. John is saying that we can call upon our Lord anytime under any circumstances and He will hear our concerns and respond in pursuit our highest good. (Look up Romans 8:28.)

* This includes LISTENING TO HIM

Look again at Verse 7, "If you abide in me, and my words abide in you, ask whatever you wish, and it will be done for you". Now this appears to be a blank check, but this is where those who have knowledge of the original language can help. The Greek word translated "words" in verse 7 is the plural form of the Greek word "rhema". Now, two Greek words are used in the New Testament to translate the phrase "word of God". The first one is

151

the word "logos" which means an objective absolute truth. The second is the word "rhema" which refers to a subjective application of truth. It is a personal spoken word applied to a specific situation.

So we abide in His presence, and as we study His objective truth in scripture, and then listen to how He takes that truth and speaks a personal word to us. And He says we must allow his Word to abide (remain) in us and to change us inside out.

* This includes PRAYING TO HIM.

In Verse 7, Jesus talks about asking for whatever you desire. This especially focuses on petitions and intercessions which involves requesting the Lord's help either in our own personal lives or in the lives of others. All through the scriptures we are encouraged to call upon the Lord and to cast our cares upon Him. but this also involves spending quality time with Him. The greatest commandment, according to Jesus in Matthew 22:36-40, is to love the Lord your God with all your heart and with all your soul and with all your mind. This calls upon us to spend quality time with God. God is not lonely, but He does delight in us. All three persons of the Trinity relate to us in unique roles. God the Father relates to us as His children. Jesus, the Son of God, relates to us as our Lord and elder brother. And the Holy Spirit relates to us as the indwelling Spirit of God who literally prompts us, counsels us, empowers us, comforts us, and changes us. They are one and yet a tri-unity.

What an exciting and incredible journey it is to spend time focusing on abiding in His presence!!

3. We must Accept His Pruning.

Look at verse 2, "Every branch in me that does not bear fruit he takes away, and every branch that does not bear fruit he prunes that it may bear more fruit." This refers to the practice of pruning a vine to improve the quantity and quality of its fruit. A vine with dead or rank twigs is less productive, and so the vinedresser takes a sharp knife and cuts away all that is unproductive. This allows the plant to conserve its energy and life, and as a result is more productive in both the quality and quantity of its fruit.

Earlier, I mentioned Galatians 5:16, which contrasts the Spirit and the flesh. Paul challenges his readers to choose to walk in the Spirit, and this will enable them to not gratify the desires of the flesh. The flesh, of course, is a reference to our old fallen nature. Note the next verse (5:17), "For the desires of the flesh are against the Spirit, and the desires of the Spirit are against the flesh, for these are opposed to each other, to keep you from doing the things you want to do." So, the old sinful nature's influence needs to be overcome through what Jesus described as a pruning.

But how does this process of pruning work? Jesus says in verse 1 that God the Father is the Vinedresser. As we attempt to abide in the Vine, The Father, who is ever present, cuts away those rank unproductive shoots that come from our old nature. And so, in addition to us resisting our old nature by abiding in Christ, the Father also counters its effect through His intervention. He does this through the Spirit by convicting us inwardly; and also by disciplining us outwardly by arranging difficult circumstances designed to get our attention. Now, as the Father prunes our lives, he does so with mercy, but not without pain.

The moment a person sincerely trusts in Jesus alone for their salvation that person is justified by faith for eternity. Simultaneously a process called sanctification begins. To be sanctified is a process which means to be set apart unto God and be made Holy as Christ is Holy. And a third step in this great salvation is called glorification. There is coming a day when we will no longer be short of His glory. When Jesus returns, He will finish what He started in our lives. In I Corinthians 15:51-52, The

Apostle Paul tells us, "Behold! I tell you a mystery…we shall be changed, in a moment, in the twinkling of an eye, at the last trumpet. For the trumpet will sound, and the dead will be raised imperishable, and we shall all be changed." So, each person reading these words who has trusted in Jesus alone for their salvation can say with assurance that **I have been justified, I am being sanctified, and someday I will be glorified.**

But until death or the rapture, the Lord continues His pruning process. And the instrument He uses, according to verse 3, is His Word. God uses the powerful truth of His Word to CONVICT us of our sin; CONVINCE us that Jesus is the Lord and Savior; CONVERT us to trust in Jesus alone for our eternal salvation; CORRECT us when we stray off the right path; and ultimately CONFORM us to the image of Christ." Hebrews 4:12 says, "The Word of God is sharper than a two-edged sword." Maybe this is why some people are hesitant to really listen to and study the Word. It confronts us with the truth, and many are afraid to face the truth about who they really are and what will happen to them at the end of their lives on this earth. Well, I want to close this study with a brief look at what happens in the lives of those who choose to commit their lives as a follower of the Lord Jesus Christ.

IV. OUR PROGRESSION IN CHRIST

In the passage I have focused on in this chapter, Jesus mentions several blessings that come to those who deeply commit to abiding in the Vine which includes abandoning to His purpose; abiding in His presence; and accepting His pruning.

1. We Will Produce More Fruit.

John 15:2, 8: "Every branch in me that does not bear fruit He takes away, and every branch that does bear fruit He prunes, that it may bear more fruit"; "by this my Father is glorified, that you bear much fruit and so prove to be my disciples."

2. We Will Experience Answered Prayer.

John 15:7, "If you abide in me, and my words abide in you, ask whatever you wish, and it will be done for you." Psalm 37:4, "Delight yourself in the Lord, and he will give the desires of your heart." Note in each of these verses, the key is that we have totally surrendered to the Lord as our Vine and our awesome God.

3. We Will Experience a Deeper Love.

John 15:9-10, 12, "As the Father has loved me, so have I loved you. Abide in my love. If you keep my commandments, you will abide in my love, just as I have kept my Father's commandments and abide in his love...This is my commandment, that you love one another as I have loved you."

Jesus loves us as the Father loves Him. And as we can continually experience this love, He enables us to love others with this same kind of love.

4. We Will Experience a Greater Joy

John 15:11, "These things I have spoken to you, that my joy might be in you, and that your joy may be full". His desire is that we will continually be filled with His joy. One of my favorite verses is Psalm 16:11 which says, "You will show me the path of life; In your presence is fullness of joy; At your right hand are pleasures forevermore."

Let us not forget the context in which Jesus was teaching these amazing truths, as He left the upper room with His disciples (minus Judas), He made His way toward Gethsemane, all along the way teaching the eleven. He told them that they would receive the Holy Spirit who would enable them to remember the things that He was teaching them.

155

What an incredible image we see here of the One who spoke to Moses from the burning bush and who identified Himself as I AM. He is making his way to the Mount of Olives to spend time in prayer in the Garden of Gethsemane to prepare Himself to fulfill His mission as the Lamb of God.

Praise the Lord Jesus for what He accomplished for us sinners who have been saved, by the power His blood, and His triumphant resurrection!

David Jeremiah shared this poem by Helen Mallicoat in his book titled "The Jesus You May Not Know".

I was regretting the past and fearing the future.
Suddenly my Lord was speaking
"My name is I AM."

He paused .....I waited.
He continued, "When you live in the past with its
Mistakes and regrets, it is hard. I am not there.
"My name is not I WAS."

When you live in the future, with its problems and
Fears, it is hard, I am not there.
"My name is not I WILL BE."

When you live in this moment,
It is not hard. I am here,
"My name is I AM."

The Conclusion

Paul Little has written that in the light of the credentials and claims about Jesus we have looked at, there are four possibilities to consider:

OPTION # 1 Was He a Liar?

Did Jesus intentionally attempt to deccive people into believing that He was the Messiah/God incarnate? I believe a careful, open-minded observation of His life reveals no deceit nor inconsistency in His life and ministry. His entire life was a model of great integrity and authenticity.

OPTION # 2 Was He a Lunatic?

Some skeptics say that Jesus was sincere, but self-deceived. In our modern times, we consider people who claim to be God, to be mentally disturbed or deranged. But an open-minded person must conclude that Jesus exhibited no signs or evidence of the imbalances and abnormalities that typically characterize people who are mentally ill. Even many skeptics agree that Jesus spoke in profound ways that would not be typical for people who are crazy or deceived.

OPTION # 3 Was He a Legend?

Some skeptics have even questioned if there ever was a historical Jesus. But today very few secular historians give credence to this view. Why? Because of the overwhelming evidence of archeology and over 5,000 Greek manuscripts of the New Testament.

F. F. Bruce, the late eminent professor at the University of Manchester, England wrote. " There is no body of ancient literature in the world which enjoys such a wealth of good textual attestation as the New

Testament." And the evidence is not just limited to the Bible. Other secular historians and writers such as Josephus, who lived during the first or second century, refer to Jesus as a historical figure. In the light of the evidence and the enduring impact of the life of Jesus, are you prepared to take Him seriously, or simply dismiss Him as a legend who has no relevance to your life today?

OPTION # 4 Was He and does He continue to be the Lord?

Yes, and since He is the Lord, then my friend, we can have hope. In the Scriptures, the word "hope" does not mean mere wishful thinking. Hope means a confident expectation about the future based on the trustworthiness of God and His Word. As the Lord over the universe, nothing is too difficult for Him. So, as the old Greyhound bus commercial used to say with a couple of alterations, "Relax, and leave the driving to the Lord!" I love Romans 15:13 which says, "Now may the God of hope fill you with all joy and peace in believing, that you may abound in hope by the power of the Holy Spirit."

As I come to the conclusion of this book, I want to emphasize again, that there is hope, or a "Blessed Assurance", for all who will repent of their sins and trust in Jesus alone for their salvation. Mark 1:14-15 tells us Jesus said, "The time is fulfilled, and the kingdom of God is at hand; repent and believe in the gospel."

This is the response Jesus still calls upon people to choose, if they desire to be a part of God's eternal kingdom. To repent and believe means to feel genuine sorrow for one's sins, and then willfully turn away from the old life of sin, and then turn to Jesus. And as you turn to Jesus confessing Him as your Lord, trusting in Him alone for His forgiveness, and receiving from Him the gift of eternal life, you can rejoice because He has promised all who do this the gift of eternal life with Jesus!

If this is something you have never done, and you desire to settle it right now, I want to share a suggested prayer that you could pray or use as guide to your words. What matters the most to the Lord is the intent of your heart.

> *Dear Lord, I come to you acknowledging that I am a sinner and that I am incapable of saving my soul. I call upon you Lord to be merciful to me a sinner. By your grace, Lord, I repent of my sins and trust in Jesus alone as my Lord and Savior. I receive from you the gift of eternal life. I ask that you crucify my old sinful self and that you enable me to live in the power of your resurrection. Thank you, Lord. AMEN*

If you have prayed this prayer with sincerity, I want to congratulate you on making the most important decision a person can ever make. I welcome you into the forever family of God. Now in John chapter three, Jesus describes this experience as being born again. So, a new convert to Christ is like a new-born baby spiritually. Just as children must grow physically, and intellectually, this is also true for those who have been born again spiritually.

Now, I want to close with some suggested practices that will enable you to grow and mature spiritually.

It is important to know that when you receive Christ, you not only receive the gift of eternal life, but you also become a disciple of Christ. A disciple is a student or learner, who follows the teachings of a Master teacher. He is our Savior but also our Lord. And as we commit to follow Him and grow, I want to use some analogies from the physical, and apply to the spiritual. 1 Peter 2:2 says, "Like newborn infants, long for the pure spiritual milk, that by it you may grow up..." To survive and be healthy physically, there are necessary practices which have similarities to spiritual growth and health.

1. Food - The Bible

2. Breathing - Prayer

3. Rest - Worship

4. Exercise - Serve (evangelize and minister)

5. Family - The Church

These are all important habits or practices that are essential to us being strong, happy and healthy children of the Living God.

It is my prayer that the Lord will use this book to either draw you to Jesus as your Lord and Savior, or if you are already a believer, that He will use it spur you on to being a fully devoted follower of Jesus as the Lord of your life. May God bless you and yours!

Acknowledgements

I am greatly indebted to several important people in my life who assisted me in the completion of this book.

First, I am so very grateful to Paul Gabriel, my good friend and fellow minister of the gospel. He amazes me with his many skills, including his ability to multi-task. He demonstrates this by serving as the senior pastor of a strong multi-cultural congregation in Columbus, Ohio; as a professor in Biblical studies at a local Bible College; and as the founder and President of FBS Publishers. Paul assisted me with my first book titled "Joseph: A Life Shaped for God's Glory." I could never have completed this second book apart from Paul's encouragement and assistance.

I also want to express my gratitude to Scott and Kim Collins, my son-in-law and daughter. I am not exactly mechanically inclined, which includes typing on a computer. I often sought Scott and Kim's help as I typed this book. They were very patient and supportive as I plucked my way to the finish line.

I had a lot of cheerleaders and prayer warriors who were aware I was working on this book. I want to mention a few who have especially expressed their support: Jeff Adams; Gene and Shane Belew; Scott Ehlers; Paul Olson; Mike Stasko; Dr. Dan Stowe; Steve Vulgamore; Jim Wallace, P. J. Wenzel, and Randall Wood.

Finally, I appreciate the patience and practical support of my precious wife Brenda. She has been, throughout many years of ministry, a great encourager and helpmate, even in those "rare" moments of my grumpiness.

Bibliography

BRISCOE, D. STUART. "Spirit Life", FLEMING H, REVELL COMPANY, 1983.

BLACKABY, HENRY T.," Experiencing God", The Sunday School Board of the SBC, 1990.

DOUGLAS, J, D, & TENNEY MERRILL C. "NIV Compact Dictionary of the Bible", ZONDERVAN PUBLISHING, 1989.

DORSETT, LYLE W. "A Passion for Souls" (The Life of D L Moody), MOODY PRESS, 1997 .

EASLEY, KEN, "In Christ", FULLNESS MAGAZINE, March-April 1981.

FREDRICKSON, ROGER L, "John" , The Communicator's Commentary. Volume 4, WORD BOOKS, 1985.

HOWARD, KEVIN & ROSENTHAL, MARVIN, 'The Feasts of the Lord", THOMAS NELSON PUBLISHERS, 1997.

HULL, WILLIAM E. The Broadman Bible Commentary, Volume 9, Luke-John, 1970.

JEREMIAH, DAVID, "The Jesus You May Not Know", TURNING POINT, 2020.

LINDSELL, HAROLD, "When You Pray", TYNDALE HOUSE PUBLISHERS, 1969.

LINDSEY, HAL, "The Liberation of Planet Earth", ZONDERVAN PUBLISHING HOUSE, 1974.

LITTLE, PAUL E. , "Know What You Believe", VICTOR BOOKS, 1985.

LITTLE, PAUL E. , "Know Why You Believe", IVP BOOKS, 2000.

MACLAREN, ALEXANDER, Expositions of Holy Scripture (St. John XV to XXI).

MACGREGOR, G. H. C, The Gospel of John, The Moffatt New Testament Commentary, HARPER AND BROTHERS PUBLISHERS.

MCDOWELL, JOSH, "More Than a Carpenter", TYNDALE HOUSE PUBLISHERS, 1977.

OGILVIE, LLOYD JOHN, "The Bush is Still Burning", WORD BOOKS, 1980.

ROGERS, ADRIAN, "The Secret of Supernatural Living", SERMON

RIDENOUR, FRITZ, "So What's the Difference?", REGAL BOOKS, 1979.

STROBEL, LEE, "The Case for Christ", ZONDERVAN BOOKS, 1998.

VINE, W.E. "Expository Dictionary of New Testament Words', FLEMING H. REVELL CO., 1966.

WESTCOTT, B. F. "The Gospel According to St. John", WM. B. EERDMANS PUBLISHING CO. 1967.

WIERSBE, WARREN W., "Real Worship: It Will Transform Your Life", OLIVER NELSON BOOKS, 1986.

WIERSBE, WARREN W., "The Wiersbe Bible Commentary (NT), DAVID C. COOK, 2007.

About the Author

Darrel Gabbard was born in Hamilton, Ohio, twenty miles north of Cincinnati. He was blessed with Christian parents, and when he was a freshman at Miami University (Ohio) experienced a strong call to be a minister of the Gospel. After graduating from Miami with a B.A. Degree, he married the love of his life, Brenda. At the time of this writing they have been married 54 years.

He then attended and graduated from The Southern Baptist Theological Seminary in 1970 with an M. Div. degree. He was pastor of five SBC churches from 1968 until his retirement in 2013. His last pastorate was at Dublin Baptist Church in Dublin, Ohio where he served for 24 plus years as Senior Pastor. Later the church elected him as Pastor Emeritus.

After retirement he continued to serve in a part time position with the Metro Columbus Baptist Association as Pastoral Encourager for 8 years. This position involved the encouragement and mentoring of younger pastors. He was also active in His denomination which included serving as a trustee for two

Southern Baptist Seminaries and as the President of the State Convention of Baptists in Ohio in 1989-1990.

God blessed Darrel and Brenda with three children: Christopher and Kevin, who are now in heaven; daughter Kimberly, who is married to Scott Collins. They also have three grandchildren which includes Samantha (Kevin's daughter); Michael and Aaron (Scott and Kimberly's sons); and three great-grandchildren. Their names are Gabriel, Micah (Michael's sons); and Jericho (Aaron's son).

Darrel currently deals with the challenges of a form of Parkinson's called Parkinsonism. But his desire to glorify God and share the gospel of Christ has not been diminished.

Made in the USA
Columbia, SC
05 September 2024

41886426R00096